DATE DUE

JUN 1 8 1968

JUL 1 0 1968

AUG 6 1968

DE R 3 W 1970

NOV 1968

MAY 8 1971

FEB 5 1969

MAY 8 1971

DEC 1 6 1969

AUG 8 1971

JAN 6 1971

the visible hand:
the fundamentals
of economic planning

the
visible
hand:
the fundamentals
of economic planning

GERALD SIRKIN
Associate Professor of Economics
The City College of
The City University of New York

McGraw-Hill Book Company

New York   St. Louis   San Francisco
Toronto   London   Sydney

The Visible Hand:
The Fundamentals
of Economic Planning

Library of Congress Catalog Card Number
67-26888

1234567890VBVB7432106987

TO MY PARENTS

There will be time, there will be time . . .
Time for you and time for me,
And time yet for a hundred indecisions,
And for a hundred visions and revisions. . . .

T. S. Eliot
"The Love Song of J. Alfred Prufrock"

preface

The Visible Hand was born in a seminar at the University of Bombay when, after I had made some critical remarks on economic policy making in India, a colleague suggested I was against planning. In answering that charge I became aware that my definition of "planning" was fuzzy, that my hosts' definition was fuzzy, and that our fuzzy definitions were not the same.

The result was continual misunderstanding. My attempt to clear up that misunderstanding has led to this study of the meaning of planning, the relation of planning to the general question of the role of government in the economy, and the comparison between planning and alternative methods of policy making.

Because the muddle about planning is so pervasive and so harmful, I have tried to make this book one which can be read not only by students of economics but also by people with little or no economic training. The general reader may strike some technical rough spots but, I believe, no impassable obstacles.

The title *The Visible Hand* is a phrase which I thought my private property until it appeared in a recent article by Egon Neuberger in the May, 1966, issue of *American Economic Review* ("Libermanism, Computopia, and Visible Hand: The Question of Informational Efficiency"). Neuberger himself discovered, after coining the phrase, that it had previously been used by Joseph S. Berliner (*Factory and Manager in the USSR*, Harvard University Press, 1957). Neuberger, however, uses it in a narrower sense than I. I mean by "the visible hand" all government substitutes for Adam Smith's "invisible hand," the free market.

I am indebted to the United States Educational Foundation in India for a Fulbright research grant in India, where this book began. I am also indebted to the Rockefeller Foundation for a grant which made possible a leave of absence to complete the writing. I have had the benefit of comments by Charles E. Lindblom, of Yale University, on the entire manuscript, and Dean W. Morse, of Columbia University, on Chapter 7, for which I am grateful. Needless to say, neither these readers nor these organizations necessarily share my views, and I am responsible for all the errors.

The efforts of my wife, Natalie P. Robinson Sirkin, to improve this book have been invaluable and unremitting.

Gerald Sirkin

contents

Preface vii

1 **THE CONFUSIONS AND ILLUSIONS OF PLANNING** 1
"Planning Means Intelligent Management" 2
"All Government Intervention in the Economy Is
Planning" 2
"The Government Is an Optimizing Machine" 3
"Planners Are Prophets" 3
Collectivist Bogies and "Laissez Fairy" Tales 4

2 **THE AGENDA OF GOVERNMENT** 7
Non-market Products 8
Efforts to Improve the Functioning of Markets 9
Information 9
Competition 10
Resource Mobility 15
Stabilization 15
Intervention to Correct Inherent Defects in the Market
Mechanism 16
Interdependence or Externalities 16
Incorrigible Consumer Ignorance or Irrationality 19
Regulation of Unavoidable Monopoly 20
Reduction of Uncertainty and Risk 20
Reallocation of Resources in Emergencies 21
Speculation 22
Hurdling the Barriers of Risk and Size 24
The Distribution of Income 26
Decreasing-cost Industries 27
International Transactions 29
Marginal Product of Labor below Subsistence Wage 30
Optimizing the Rate of Saving 31

APPENDIX TO CHAPTER 2
The Optimum Rate of Saving 33

3 "PLANNING"—A WORD IN SEARCH OF A MEANING 43

A Precise Definition of "Planning" 45
What Planning Is Not 47
Economic Organization and Planning 51
    Price versus Non-price Systems 51
    Private versus Public Ownership 53
    Centralized versus Decentralized Planning 53
    Total versus Partial Planning 53

Summary 54

4 GOVERNMENT IN THE ECONOMY: PORTRAIT WITH WARTS 55

The Rules of the Private Game 56
The Public Warts 57
    The Clash of Objectives 58
    The Criteria of Performance 61
    Government Antipathy to Competition and Diversity 62
    Uncertainty and Risk Taking 64
    Irrationality 65
    Corruption 66
Secondary Warts 67
    The Impossibility of Complete Centralization 68
    Central Control and the Price System 69
    The Middle Morass 71
    The Information Gap 72
    The Failure in International Exchange 74
    The Forecasting Fallacies 75

5 PLANNING IN DEVELOPED COUNTRIES 79

Land-use Planning 79
Private-enterprise Planning à la Mode Continentale 90
    France 90
    The Netherlands 94
    Others 94
Public-enterprise Planning, Yugoslav Style 95
The Soviet Style 97
    Growth Despite Planning 102

6 GOVERNMENT IN BACKWARD AND UNDERDEVELOPED ECONOMIES 115

Backwardness and Underdevelopment 115
The Attack on Backwardness 117
    Entrepreneurship 119
    Land Reform and Entrepreneurship 122
    Population Control 122
The Attack on Underdevelopment 123
    Accelerating Capital Formation 123

Balanced Growth 125
Limitations of Government 130

7 PLANNING FOR DEVELOPMENT: INDIA 133
What Kind of Planning? 133
The Strategy of Indian Planning 137
  The Main Objectives 137
  The Constraints 139
Strategy in Theory 141
Strategy in Practice 145
The Plan and the Market 153
Public versus Private Enterprise 161
Lessons of the Indian Experience 166

8 GUIDELINES FOR THE VISIBLE HAND 169
Index 183

1 | the confusions and illusions of planning

I am perennially saddened by the never-ending
yearning for an "over-all plan"—that wonderful,
permanent ordering of people, money, space,
and buildings, in which everyone will have an
Eames chair, a parking space, and the trains will
always, always run on time.[1]

The idea of planning springs from the yearning of
fastidious minds for an orderly, coordinated, errorless
conduct of society's affairs. Yet nothing better illustrates the contrast between this ideal of perfect order
and the reality of man's methods than the muddle
which surrounds the concept of planning itself. It has
evidently been necessary to pass through an extended
phase of confused discussion and practical experience to approach a clear understanding of what planning means and how it works. The process of clarification, however, is only beginning. To see how
much remains to be done we need only look at five $\longrightarrow$
fundamental confusions that are still prevalent.

[1] Arthur D. Trottenberg, Assistant Dean of the Faculty of Arts
and Sciences for Resources and Planning, Harvard University, *Harvard Alumni Bulletin*, Nov. 7, 1964.

"planning means intelligent management"

Mr. Nehru described planning as an exercise of human intelligence in dealing with facts and situations as they were and trying to find a way to solve problems. He, therefore, could not understand how even the few who refused to accept the principles of planning, or rather the backward few, could disagree with planning in an intelligent way which could be understood by intelligent people.[2]

This typical statement by Nehru exemplifies a common obscurantic use of the word "planning." If "planning" is used to mean the intelligent solving of economic problems, its use is noncontroversial and sweetly reasonable at the expense of saying practically nothing. All managers of economic activities try to be intelligent "in dealing with facts and situations" and in "trying to find a way to solve problems." But "planning" is not synonymous with intelligent management; it refers—rather, it *should* refer—to certain specific methods of managing an economy. Until the essential characteristics of planning are identified, no clear discussion of the subject can take place.

"all government intervention in the economy is planning"

In popular usage any government economic function is likely to be called "planning":

Opponents of the planned society may balk at this [compulsory arbitration]; but in fact great areas of planning and control, from traffic lights to the Federal Reserve System, are already the lubricants of our complex civilization. . . .[3]

[2] Report of a speech by Jawaharlal Nehru, *The Times of India,* Aug. 23, 1960, p. 7.
[3] Letter to the editor of *The New York Times,* Jan. 8, 1966.

Governments do planning, but everything governments do is not planning. To make the distinction, a clear definition of planning is needed.

"the government is an optimizing machine"

Much of the misunderstanding about planning can be traced to the propensity of economists to detach the economic analysis of planning from any consideration of the nature of the government which is to do the planning. The analysis ordinarily proceeds: If the government does thus and so, then the economy will be closer to an optimum. But little or no attention is paid to whether it is in the nature of governments to do thus and so.

We are all familiar with examples of government malpractice in the economy, but these alone carry little conviction. "For instance is not an argument," runs the old Bronx proverb. To be convinced that economic analysis is invalid which is based on the assumption that the government is an optimizing machine, one must understand why certain shortcomings of government economic policy and administration are *inherent* in the operations of government.

"planners are prophets"

Another all-too-readily accepted proposition about planning is that it confers upon the planners unusual powers to foresee the future. Consider these statements about planning:

> Just as there is an extension of the field of cognition over the breadth of industry, so also is there an increase in the length of foresight in time. A Central Authority can take account of processes which are occurring so slowly, or will begin to occur so far in the future, that no single producer could be aware of their existence.[4]

[4] E. F. M. Durbin, *Problems of Economic Planning* (London: Routledge & Kegan Paul, Ltd., 1949), p. 51.

What is this mysterious prophetic vision that comes to a man when he sits at a desk in the central authority but not when he sits at a desk in a business or university?

> And it is to be hoped that these countries, since they have long-term plans, will disclose projections of their probable demand for primary commodities, so as to enable producing countries to base their policy decisions on sounder foundations than they have been able to do to date.[5]

Do the long-term projections of plans really provide "sounder foundations" for policy? What would have happened to a primary-producing country which, having committed itself on the basis of the projections of the Soviet Union and its satellites in 1960, then faced the disappointments and revisions of those countries' plans in the succeeding five years?

collectivist bogies and "laissez-fairy" tales

The discussion of planning has been befogged by the suspicions of some that most government interventions are steps toward collectivism and by the allegations of others that strict critics of government intervention are extremists pursuing the impossible goal of *laissez faire*. The basic cause of this confusion is that the parties have not evolved a set of principles by which they can distinguish the government policies which they find acceptable from those they find unacceptable. Consequently, they have been prone to praise or condemn the general idea of government economic policy, unable to make the kind of distinction among policies that would prevent the appearance of extremism.[6] This is not to

---

[5] Raúl Prebisch, "Commercial Policy in the Underdeveloped Countries," *American Economic Review*, vol. 49, no. 2 (May, 1959), pp. 265–266.
[6] Note, for example, this statement, with its implications that the "free-enterprise" position in the United States advocates total *laissez faire* and that all the policies mentioned are, in principle, equally good evidence

say that agreement on a set of principles for classifying government policies will end the debate, but it will certainly clarify it.

The classification of government policies will also shed light on the controversy over the relation of economic policy to personal freedom. For example, clearly relevant is the distinction between policies which can be administered by general and impersonal rules and policies which require the administrators to make discretionary choices. To the extent that the preservation of personal freedom depends upon the limitation of arbitrary government power, the ranking of government economic policies according to their generality and impartiality is an important criterion in assessing those policies.

At what point the concentration of economic power in the hands of the government becomes a danger to personal freedom is not a question that can be answered. The dispersion of economic power is one of the defenses of freedom, though not, by itself, a guarantee of freedom. Economic independence makes possible the dissent and criticism which constantly curb government power. Economic independence stimulates the outspokenness and diversity of the medium of dissent and criticism—the press.

In countries lacking a tradition of personal freedom from government coercion and without a well-established democratic process, the dispersion of economic power is particularly important for the evolution of freedom and democratic government. In countries having a tradition of personal freedom and democracy, the danger of the government's abuse of its economic power is undoubtedly much less. Nevertheless, there are limits to the protection that tradition and democracy can

---

that private enterprise needs to be fettered: "Legislation regarding trusts, cartels and monopolies, farm price supports, tariffs, subsidies to shipping and ship-building and more recently to railroads, the Buy American Act, policies to prevent recession from deteriorating into depression and for combatting inflation, measures for providing employment through state expenditure—all these are evidence of practical limitations to the operation of *unfettered* private enterprise. . . ." G. L. Mehta, "As Others See Us: An Indian View," *Foreign Affairs*, vol. 37, no. 1 (October, 1958), p. 113.

provide. In a time of unusual stress—the McCarthyist period in the United States—it was the decentralization of economic power, far more than the traditions of freedom and democracy, that mitigated the abuse of individuals.

The political implications of the dispersion of economic power are imprecise, and in some quarters subject to exaggeration, but they do suggest this much: The dispersion of economic power is a valuable asset to society, and its diminution is one of the costs of certain types of government economic intervention. These costs must be weighed against the potential gains of such interventions. An economic policy, to be defensible, must promise not merely *some* economic improvement, but an improvement sufficiently large and certain to justify the concomitant sacrifice, if any, of the dispersion of economic power.

These confusions about what planning is are part of a larger set of misunderstandings about how economic decisions, both private and governmental, are actually made and about the problems of implementing economic decisions. From these misunderstandings there arises, not only a pitifully exaggerated idea of the economic wonders that governments can perform, but a fundamental misconception of the way governments ought to go about making their economic decisions. The clarification of the issues of planning entails, therefore, some review of the broader questions of how governments and private units make economic decisions and carry them out and of the bases for dividing the administration of the economy between the private and the public sectors. This review is presented in Chapter 2 to provide the foundation for the discussion, in Chapter 3, of what planning means.

2 | the agenda of government

Seventy-three years ago Beatrice Webb, commenting in her diary on the debates over the role of the state in the economy, and confident that the issue would be settled somewhere between the extremes, wrote:

> The controversy which seems to us now so full of significance and import will seem barren and useless to our great-grandchildren; they will be amazed that we fought so hard to establish one metaphysical position and to destroy another.[1]

More than a generation later Keynes was writing:

> We cannot therefore settle on abstract grounds, but must handle on its merits in detail what Burke termed "one of the finest problems in legislation, namely, to determine what the State ought to take upon itself to direct by the public wisdom, and what it ought to leave, with as little interference as possible, to individual exertion." We have to discriminate between what Bentham, in his forgotten but useful nomenclature, used to term *Agenda* and *Non-Agenda*. . . . Perhaps the chief task of Economists at this hour is to

[1] Beatrice Webb, *Our Partnership,* ed. by Barbara Drake and Margaret I. Cole (London: Longmans, Green & Co., Ltd., 1948), p. 118.

distinguish afresh the *Agenda* of Government from the *Non-Agenda*. . . .[2]

Today finds the great-grandchildren of the Webbs' generation not at all amazed that they fought so hard, but rather, like Keynes, observing that distinguishing the Agenda from the Non-Agenda is a vital and continuous task for economists. If anything, the need for clarification of the question is greater today than when Mrs. Webb made her prediction, for since then all countries have cut loose from the ideal of a minimum government Agenda, and most have retained their doubts about adopting the other extreme, so that, drifting in between, they commit costly and even tragic errors, through both what they include and what they exclude from the Agenda.

To arrive at some satisfactory formula by which we can divide all proposals for state action into those that a wise society will put on the Agenda and those it will leave off—in Keynes's words, to settle the matter "on abstract grounds"—is a vain hope. We must "handle on its merits in detail" the problem of what should be done by the state and what by the individual. But we can hope to arrive at some principles which will be generally acceptable to free men to guide us in our decisions as we examine in detail the merits of each proposal.

Let us begin by reviewing the bases for government participation or intervention in the economy. The rather large number of propositions can be grouped under four general headings.

NON-MARKET PRODUCTS

A private economy must operate through a market system in which goods are bought and sold. Certain products, however, cannot be exchanged in markets. Any product whose enjoyment or benefit will be shared by the members of the society,

---

[2] John Maynard Keynes, *The End of Laissez-faire* (London: Leonard & Virginia Woolf at The Hogarth Press, Ltd., 1926), p. 40.

whether they choose to make a payment for it or not, will obviously not be produced for sale. National defense and police protection are examples.[3] Parks, roads, and aids to navigation are other examples. (Conceivably access to these facilities could be controlled, as in the case of toll roads, and the services sold; but in general the considerations of cost and practicality require that such services be provided outside the market.) Flood control and sanitation are still other examples of services which, by their nature, must be produced and used collectively.

EFFORTS TO IMPROVE THE FUNCTIONING OF MARKETS [4]

Certain imperfections in the organization and operation of markets are capable of at least partial correction by government action. The principle of government intervention to improve the workings of the market has always been accepted by intelligent advocates of a market system, though the precise methods and the limits are properly subjects for debate. The ways in which the state can make a contribution toward a better working of markets fall into four categories: information, competition, resource mobility, and stabilization.

information

Perfect decision making requires perfect information, whether in a market or a non-market system. In no system can there ever be perfect information, but where a government is concerned about the quality of its economic performance, it must,

---

[3] Since order and justice require that the power of coercion be a state monopoly, these services would have to be produced by the government in any event.

[4] I shall assume that readers are familiar with the mechanism of a market system, i.e., a system in which individuals are free to buy and sell inputs and outputs, guided by their own objectives and preferences and by the structure of relative prices, which, in turn, are free to change in response to the market decisions of individuals.

9

weighing the gains against the costs, consider measures to raise the level of information available to the decision makers.

Buyers of consumer goods need to know the prices and the quality of the available products. Buyers of inputs need similar data. Sellers need information about the prices and conditions prevailing in the various markets. Buyers' and sellers' decisions will be improved if they have this information for future markets as well as for present markets.

Much of the desired information in a developed market system becomes available without the aid of the state. In particular, businesses can undertake to gather or buy market data, although for small businesses, such as farms, the private sources of market information may be inadequate. The chief problems, however, arise for consumers, labor, and investors, for whom certain types of information are extremely costly or impossible to obtain. The consumers' difficulty is insufficient knowledge of the quality of products which they are not equipped to analyze. Hence the government may set standards, impose labeling requirements, or regulate against dishonest advertising. Labor's knowledge of labor markets can be increased by the government's publishing information or organizing labor exchanges. Investors may be assisted by regulations requiring the disclosure of reliable information about companies whose securities are sold in security markets. The government may also attempt to increase the supply of information about future markets, though whether in general it can improve on private forecasts is doubtful.[5]

competition

The defective functioning of markets that results from imperfect competition is a familiar and much-analyzed matter, as is the effort to preserve or increase competition by attacking bigness or prohibiting practices that restrain or reduce competition. The propriety of a government program to promote competition in a private-enterprise economy hardly requires an ideological defense. But a related theme—the alleged futility of a program to promote competition—needs investigation. Is

[5] See next chapter.

the attempt to maintain or increase competition so hopeless and pointless that it has no place among government economic policies?

The disparagement of pro-competition policies arises primarily from the view that, since the conditions of pure competition are unattainable for technological reasons, the inevitability of imperfect competition in a large part of the economy renders fruitless the effort to preserve and extend competition. This position constitutes an extreme exaggeration of the monopoly problem.

Even in the case of a so-called natural monopoly, where by reasons of technology and the size of the market greatest efficiency can be achieved by allotting the entire market to a single firm, a considerable element of competition is always present. Inter-product competition always exists, since, in the last analysis, every product is a substitute for all others in the buyer's budget. Generally, inter-product competition is quite close. In the case of steel, substitutes like aluminum, concrete, and plastic are proving to be keen competitors, and others are being developed. Railroads have road, air, and water transportation to compete with. It is difficult to think of a product that does not have at least one close substitute, and even there competition exists in less obvious ways. An electric power company is subject to the competition of other power companies in so far as the location of customers will be affected by relative rates.

The number of cases where technological efficiency requires one firm only in an industry is still quite small in the modern economy. Inflated notions of economies of scale have given rise to the popular belief that a substantial part of manufacturing requires high concentration of production and that the trend is in the direction of complete concentration. Studies of optimum size indicate that in many United States industries having high concentration, the degree of concentration is not dictated by economies of scale.[6] Investigations of the long-run

[6] See Joe S. Bain, "Economies of Scale, Concentration, and the Condition of Entry in Twenty Manufacturing Industries," *American Economic Review*, vol. 44, no. 1 (March, 1954), pp. 15–39. The optimum scale of plant, as estimated by engineering studies in twenty industries,

behavior of concentration in the United States fail to reveal any upward trend.[7]

Thus, both inter-industry and intra-industry competition are almost always present to restrain monopoly power. Other restraints can also be cited. International competition limits monopoly power in most products. There is, moreover, the unseen but powerful deterrent of *potential* competition: competition in the form of new entrants to an industry or new products to compete with the old which will be attracted should the profits of the existing firms become abnormally high.[8] Should all other restraints on monopolistic positions be lacking, fear of government regulation will usually discourage overexploitation.

There is, therefore, a substantial contribution which government anti-monopoly policy can make. This policy can be directed toward (1) preventing the merging of competing industries (for example, the control of motor transportation by railroads), (2) preventing the merger of firms or ordering the partition of large firms where economies of scale do not justify the proposed or existing combinations, (3) prohibiting practices which block the entry of new firms or the introduction of new products, (4) prohibiting specific practices which restrain competition (discriminatory pricing, tied sales), (5) prosecuting collusive agreements or arrangements, (6) opening the domestic market to foreign competition, (7) discontinuing the government's own anti-competition practices (licensing to re-

---

was found to permit a fairly large number of such plants in the United States national market. For example, a single optimum-sized plant would produce the following percentage of its industry's output: in steel, 1 to 2½; in rubber tires and tubes, 3; in soap, 4 to 6; in automobiles, 5 to 10. Furthermore, the economies of *multiplant* firms appear to be nil in most of the industries studied and quite small in the others.

[7] G. Warren Nutter, *The Extent of Enterprise Monopoly in the United States, 1899–1939* (Chicago: The University of Chicago Press, 1951); Henry A. Einhorn, "Enterprise Monopoly and the Concentration of Domestic Industrial Output: 1939–1958," Ph.D. dissertation, New York: Columbia University, 1963.

[8] Except where government bars it, new firms have managed to batter their way into established markets or to devise substitute products in most industries offering unusual profits.

strict entry, aid and encouragement in the formation of cartels, restrictions on regional trade, laws to help fix prices).

These policies, it is true, will not establish pure competition. Except where each firm's share of the market is so small that the firm has no influence over the price of its product, firms will not behave like pure competitors. The practical question, however, is: How significant for economic welfare is the difference between pure competition and the kind of competition which can be sustained by government policy?

To answer this question, one must recall the objections to monopoly. The classical argument is that the monopolist keeps the price of his product above the marginal cost of producing it and restricts his output to less than the optimum quantity.

The extent to which this misallocation of production occurs will obviously depend on the elasticity of demand for the monopolized product. Given the competition between industries, the potential competition of new firms and new products, and the threat of competition from abroad, a producer will rarely be able to believe that elasticity of demand for his product is low enough to give him much monopoly power, even if he can disregard rivals in his own industry. Where there is competition within the industry, as frequently happens, the monopolist (or, more accurately, the oligopolist) has even less power to raise prices and restrict production. All in all, it is difficult to believe that when the government undertakes to preserve the feasible degree of competition, sufficient monopoly power survives to permit more than a trivial misallocation of resources.

There is, however, another and stronger case against monopoly than the misallocation of resources. Competition is a driving force in the economy, impelling the entrepreneur to seek improvements, to introduce innovations, to experiment, to take risks. True enough, there are incentives for the monopolist to do those things also and there is sufficient evidence that they do, to a degree. But there is also sufficient evidence that entrepreneurs share the human trait of enjoying security, of relaxing when sheltered, of letting well enough alone. The world's economic history is replete with cases of firms which achieve what they believe to be a secure position and drift into a prolonged period of technical and managerial stagnation until (and unless) they are shaken by the emergence of competition.[9]

The type of competition required to maintain the dynamic propulsion of entrepreneurs is not *pure* competition. Competition among industries, competition among oligopolists in the same industry, the threat of new products—all will do as well. Among firms that may be wary of direct price competition, competition through the search for better products and methods goes on vigorously as long as there is a danger that someone else, in the industry or outside it, may steal a march. Genuine security from innovational competition is possible only when the government guarantees it or when the government fails to break up a wholly unnecessary system of extensive monopolistic control of markets.

There is no substitute for competition as an economic propellant. Public ownership may attack (with uncertain success) the minor problem of misallocation under imperfect competition; but, by creating a total (public) monopoly, it worsens the major problem of managerial anesthesia to which the public monopolist is susceptible no less than the private.[10]

---

[9] A contrary view frequently heard is that less competition means more technological progress because of the gigantic scale required for modern research. The more this subject is investigated, the more this view appears to be a myth. See, for example, D. Hamberg, "Invention in the Industrial Research Laboratory," *Journal of Political Economy*, vol. 71, no. 2 (April, 1963), pp. 95–115. The evidence reviewed there reveals that large industrial laboratories are only minor sources of major inventions, since such laboratories devote themselves primarily to the search for the minor "improvement" inventions. The major inventions, which we have been told require the vast resources of giant corporations, turn out to emanate mostly from small firms and independent laboratories or inventors.

[10] I shall pass over, without extended discussion, an alternative view of policy with respect to competition: that competition is injurious or inefficient, and therefore the appropriate policy is to encourage monopoly. Competition is alleged to cause (1) depressed incomes to factors employed in competitive industries; (2) fluctuations of production; (3) the wastes of selling costs; (4) the waste of a shared resource, such as oil pumped from a common pool by several firms; (5) the loss

resource mobility

The movement of resources between alternative uses is essential to the efficiency of any economy subject to growth and change. In a market economy, where movement is achieved by the inducement of rewards rather than by compulsion, particular watch must be kept for situations in which movement is seriously impeded. Policies intended to increase mobility may involve the spread of information, the retraining of labor, and the removal of artificial barriers created by government or special-interest groups.

stabilization

The function of the market is to direct the allocation of inputs to alternative outputs. The market, however, does not assure that the sum of these allocations will continuously equal the total supply of inputs. When the demand for inputs exceeds the total, the allocative function of the market is impaired, since, during an inflationary phase, when prices are not clearing the market, the price mechanism by which the market determines allocation is not fully operative. When demand falls short of the total supply of inputs, the most serious misallocation, the failure to allocate some inputs to any productive use at all, occurs. Public policies aimed at stabilizing aggregate demand at the "full-employment" level through monetary or compensatory fiscal measures are not substitutes for the market system, but are efforts to improve the functioning of the market.

---

of income to a nation that does not exploit its foreign market by monopolistic selling or buying.

Objections 1 and 2 are not supported by economic analysis. Objection 3 is a minor item which has been much exaggerated by failure to distinguish it from the substantial portion of selling effort which is *not* a waste. Objection 4 is a legitimate, though infrequent, difficulty which calls for regulation (see page 17 below). Objection 5 is a boomerang: Monopolization in foreign markets either invites new competition and product substitution or else foreign retaliatory policies.

INTERVENTION TO CORRECT INHERENT DEFECTS IN THE MARKET MECHANISM

Certain defects of the market mechanism cannot be repaired, and the effort to prevent the misallocations that result must proceed by supplementing the market with direct government intervention.

interdependence or externalities

Much of the criticism of the market system stems from a common cause: Market prices may not correctly measure costs or gains to society, even if the market functions perfectly, because some costs or gains occur *outside* the market. An individual maximizing his private welfare in a market system bases his calculations only on his costs and gains in the market. When there is non-market interdependence between individuals, so that one man's actions impose costs on others which he does not pay for, or bestow gains on others for which he is not reimbursed, there is a divergence between private and social calculation.

Interdependence among consumers exists when one individual's consumption yields free enjoyment to other consumers or when it imposes costs on other consumers over and above the cost of inputs absorbed in the consumption. A handsome house or garden may confer pleasure on other members of the community. Unfortunately, it may also arouse such feelings of envy as to spread dissatisfaction. Aside from interdependence through envy, the chief examples of consumer interdependence are the creation of noise, dirt, or other annoyances to neighbors.

Direct interdependence between consumers and producers occurs when producers' actions affect individuals' satisfaction outside the market. Pollution of air or water, outdoor advertising, and damage by producers to the attractiveness of residential neighborhoods are the most important examples.

Interdependence among producers results in what are generally called *external economies* or *diseconomies*.[11] External economies are benefits (outside the market) accruing to producers as the result of the efforts or outlays of another producer. External diseconomies are non-market costs imposed on producers by the efforts or outlays of another producer.

External economies occur when a producer shares freely in some resource created by another producer. A firm which trains labor that is then employed by other firms is creating an external economy for the other firms. Research accomplishments by a firm which become freely available to other firms—basic research which cannot be patented—is another example. It is rather difficult to think of further examples unless one resorts to trivial cases like the beekeeper whose bees perform a free pollination service for neighboring farmers.[12]

External diseconomies occur when producers draw upon the same free resource, so that the cost imposed when one producer expands his use of the resource, or exploits it wastefully, falls upon other producers, but not upon the user through the market cost of the resource. Producers pumping from the same pool of oil and those fishing or gathering oysters from common waters are examples. The number of examples is limited because the number of scarce resources which are free is limited.[13]

An interdependence of a different kind among producers,

---

[11] For an excellent discussion, see Tibor Scitovsky, "Two Concepts of External Economies," *Journal of Political Economy,* vol. 62, no. 2 (April, 1954), pp. 143–151.

[12] James E. Meade, "External Economies and Diseconomies in a Competitive Situation," *Economic Journal,* vol. 62, no. 1 (March, 1952), pp. 54–67.

[13] External diseconomies are the basis for "conservation" regulations. The popular notion that regulations are needed to conserve resources for some future date is incorrect. The threat of increasing scarcity of a resource in the future is reflected in a rise in the current price. The price thus regulates the rate of consumption and distributes its use as optimally through time as human knowledge permits. Unless the cost of the resources is external to the user, the price system regulates its use at least as well as a conservation commission can.

which Scitovsky [14] has called (by stretching the meaning of the term somewhat) an external economy, occurs when the expansion of one industry (A) enlarges the market of another industry (B), thus permitting industry B to expand. The expansion of industry B increases the market for industry A and in turn permits industry A to expand. These interdependencies are expressed *through* the market, not outside it; but, it is argued, in the case of investment decisions the data of the market do not provide the same reliable guidance that they provide for other decisions. "Market prices . . . reflect the economic situation as it is and not as it will be," [15] giving proper information for current production decisions but not for investment. Investment must be related to future conditions. As a result, industries A and B may not expand so much as they would if their investment decisions were made jointly and their interdependence were internal, rather than external.

The proposition that market interdependence is necessarily a barrier to correct investment decisions is derived from a mistaken conception of entrepreneurial calculation. Private investment decisions are based, not on the present structure of the economy, but on expectations about the future. For example, in the early days of railroad building in the United States, railroad expansion was based, not on the then-existing demand for transportation, but on the demand that it would itself create. In effect, industry A foresees that if it expands, industry B will expand; and B has similar foresight about the effects of its expansion on A. Moreover, each industry does not operate in an informational vacuum; industries which are interdependent can and do communicate with each other about the interactions of their investment programs.

The problem of market interdependence is thus entirely different from the problem created by genuine externalities (non-market interdependence). Non-market interdependence leads to defective market decisions which can be corrected only by government intervention in the market. Market interdependence leads to defective decisions only to the extent that

[14] *Op. cit.*
[15] *Ibid.*, p. 150.

information and foresight are inadequate.[16] Better information, rather than intervention in the market, is required.

incorrigible consumer ignorance or irrationality

In an earlier section I discussed efforts to improve the operation of the market through increasing consumer information or knowledge. There remains the problem of attempting to reduce the loss of welfare that occurs either because information cannot be perfect or because consumers, even when supplied with correct information, make economic decisions which detract from their welfare. In certain areas of consumption, such as medical treatment and drugs, the consumers' inability to acquire expertise and the danger of their proneness to error have led to general acceptance of limitations on the consumers' and producers' choice. In general, however, there is good reason for skepticism about the possibilities of improving consumer welfare by substituting official for private judgment.

The case for intervention is clearest when there are external costs attached to consumers' "mistakes." Overindulgence in intoxicants is an example, though the disastrous consequences of prohibition, including the corruption of the law enforcers, the stimulus to other crime, and the added attraction bestowed on drinking by forbidding it, also make it an example of the difficulties of increasing welfare by limiting consumer sovereignty.

The issue of limiting consumer choice because of consumers' propensity to err has its greatest significance in the case of the choice between consumption and saving. It is alleged that consumers are prone to consume more and save less than a rational choice would dictate in the light of the relative satisfactions of present and future consumption and the increased future consumption which would be made possible by present saving. The failure of the individual to maximize his own life-

[16] See J. A. Stockfisch, "External Economies, Investment, and Foresight," *Journal of Political Economy*, vol. 63, no. 5 (October, 1955), pp. 446–449; and Tibor Scitovsky, "A Reply," *ibid.*, pp. 450–451.

time satisfaction may be due to a lack of foresight which leads him to overvalue present consumption relative to future consumption. The public must then be protected from its own misjudgment (so the argument goes) by government intervention to raise the rate of saving.[17]

regulation of unavoidable monopoly

When an industry has economies of scale which prohibit the existence of several competing firms and when inelasticity of demand for the product confers substantial monopoly power on the industry, some form of regulation intended to bring price and output closer to the competitive optimum may be undertaken.

reduction of uncertainty and risk

The risks confronting one producer because of his uncertainty about what other producers intend to do can be reduced by better dissemination of information about the intentions of the other producers.[18] The government may contribute to the supply of this information. Since risk is a cost, anything which serves to reduce risk will increase economic welfare.

Government measures to reduce risk by improving information must be distinguished from measures which merely shift the burden of risk from private to public shoulders without actually reducing the amount of risk, or which reduce risk by retarding change. If the government assumes the burden of risk by taking on the functions of entrepreneurship, the public entrepreneur either includes the risk in his calculations (with the same effects as under private entrepreneurship) or he neglects these costs, with unfortunate effects on the quality of

---

[17] A special problem arises in the case of saving by one generation to benefit succeeding generations. It can scarcely be called irrational or erroneous if an individual chooses to consume his entire income by the end of his life, that is, to have zero lifetime saving. Some other basis than error by the consumer is required to justify government imposition of consumer sacrifices on one generation for the benefit of the next.

[18] See p. 91 for an illustration.

his decisions. If the private entrepreneur remains in control, but the government bears the risk, the entrepreneur can omit the risk cost from his calculations, with obvious uneconomic consequences.

Most economic risk arises from uncertainty about change, which is part of the adjustment or development process of the economy. By preventing or slowing down adjustments in prices or reallocation of resources or innovation, the government can diminish uncertainty and risk, but at a cost to society which can rarely be worth the gain.

reallocation of resources in emergencies

It is generally thought that the price system acts too slowly to be relied on when a large reallocation of resources must be carried out rapidly. The problem of wartime mobilization of resources is the chief, if not the sole, example. Government intervention to supplement or replace the price mechanism will then be demanded.[19]

Whether the price system is, in fact, slower than government controls in mobilizing resources for war is not obvious. It is significant that free societies have not felt compelled to use direct controls to reallocate nonmilitary labor during wars. The supplanting of the price system in an emergency may reflect not its relative slowness, but the reluctance of the society to enact the strict monetary and fiscal measures required to permit the large changes in relative prices that would be necessary to carry out the reallocation. Indeed, direct controls may be slower than the price system in some respects. They may be adopted not because of, but in spite of, their effect on speed and efficiency, to avoid harsh fiscal measures and an unpopular redistribution of income.

Nevertheless, there remains a possibility which one cannot reject that certain parts of the mobilization job can be accelerated by direct controls.

[19] See James E. Meade, *Planning and the Price Mechanism* (London: George Allen & Unwin, Ltd., 1949); Lionel Robbins, *The Economic Problem in Peace and War* (London: Macmillan & Co., Ltd., 1947), pp. 29–42.

speculation

Suspicion of speculation is widespread, especially in the less developed economies, and frequently leads to proposals to regulate or even prohibit speculation.

The subject is one which deserves careful examination, since speculation is by and large a useful economic activity. It increases the volume of transactions in markets, which facilitates sales and purchases of assets. It creates a body of specialists who will assume the burden of risk, enabling those who wish to avoid risk to do so. Most important, speculation will generally have a stabilizing effect on price, because speculators aim to buy when the price is low (relative to future price) and sell when the price is high.

There is, however, the possibility that speculation may be destabilizing. Speculators may, in the aggregate, make mistaken forecasts, buying when prices are higher than they will be in the future or selling when prices are lower. Because mistakes will cause them losses, there is a presumption that if they make profits, the net effect of their activities is stabilizing.

This argument has been used for an indirect demonstration that speculation is stabilizing, since speculation would not continue unless it were profitable.[20] Several attempts have been made to demonstrate that speculation can be both destabilizing and profitable, but the presumption in favor of the stabilizing effect of speculation does not appear to be seriously shaken.[21]

[20] See Milton Friedman, "The Case for Flexible Exchange Rates," in his *Essays in Positive Economics* (Chicago: The University of Chicago Press, 1953), pp. 174–177.

[21] William J. Baumol, "Speculation, Profitability, and Stability," *Review of Economics and Statistics*, vol. 39, no. 3 (August, 1957), pp. 263–271, undertakes to present a case in which speculation, while profitable, would nevertheless have a destabilizing effect. In answer to this demonstration, Lester G. Telser, "A Theory of Speculation Relating Profitability and Stability," *ibid.*, vol. 41, no. 3 (August, 1959), pp. 295–301, argues that profitable speculation cannot be destabilizing. The difference between the two analyses hinges on which parties in the market

A frequent complaint about speculators is that they enrich themselves at the expense of farmers, by buying agricultural products at harvest time, when prices are low, and selling when prices are higher. Farmers, lacking capital to store the products themselves, must sell cheaply when they harvest the crop, and speculators reap the gains of the subsequent higher prices.

To examine the validity of this complaint, consider first the results when there is competition among buyers. Buyers bid up the price they pay farmers to the point where the margin

---

are to be considered speculators and which, nonspeculators. (See W. J. Baumol, "Reply," *ibid.*, pp. 301–302.)

M. J. Farrell, "Profitable Speculation," *Economica*, new series, vol. 33, no. 130 (May, 1960), pp. 183–193, demonstrates that in a two-period example (the speculator does all his buying in one period and all his selling in a second period), profitable speculation must be stabilizing; but that if the transactions occur in more than two periods, the speculation may be destabilizing and profitable.

However, the greater-than-two-period case can be viewed as a series of two-period transactions in which the profitable ones are stabilizing and the destabilizing ones are unprofitable. If the demand curve for the commodity is the right shape, the whole set of transactions may yield a net profit and yet increase the variance of price relative to the variance that would have occurred in the absence of speculation. Nevertheless, the profits of the speculators would be even greater if their effect were stabilizing.

A special case of profitable destabilizing speculation is possible if the speculation shifts the underlying supply and demand curves. It has been suggested that this may occur in a foreign-exchange market with flexible exchange rates. Suppose that speculation against the local currency drives down its price and thereby raises the price of imports and exports in terms of local currency. The rise of these prices may set off a general wage and price increase which will lower the equilibrium position of the exchange rate to the level where speculation pushed it. Thus speculators may destabilize the exchange rate and, in the process, may reduce the equilibrium rate so that the outcome is profitable to them. [See Jacob Viner, "Some International Aspects of Economic Stabilization," in Leonard D. White (ed.), *The State of the Social Sciences* (Chicago: The University of Chicago Press, 1956).] Note, however, that this outcome depends crucially on the process which generates a general wage and price increase when the exchange rate falls. If the general wage and price increase should not occur (and it is by no means clear that it will), the destabilizing speculation would be unprofitable.

between the buying price and the expected resale price will just cover transportation and storage costs including a normal return on capital. If farmers stored their products themselves, they would incur the same costs as traders, or higher. Therefore their net selling price would under competitive conditions be no greater than if they stored the harvest themselves. Exploitation of farmers by traders, therefore, occurs only if traders buy under monopsonistic (noncompetitive) conditions. Whether monopsony is a common phenomenon when traders buy from farmers is a question that requires more investigation. However, the few empirical studies which have been made in countries where monopsony might be expected suggest it is comparatively rare.[22]

In any event, the problem which needs correction is not speculation. Storing the products when they are plentiful to sell them when they are scarce is clearly a useful activity. It is, rather, monopsony power, if it is present, which needs correcting.

hurdling the barriers of risk and size

Imagine an economic venture which meets the standard of an efficient allocation of resources and which can be sufficiently profitable to justify a private undertaking. Is it possible that private enterprise might fail to attempt the venture because the risks or the requisite size are "too great"?

With regard to the obstacle of risk, take first the case in which entrepreneurs correctly evaluate the degree of risk. Risk is a genuine cost which must be covered if the project is to be

[22] See, for example, Mahar Mangahas, Aida E. Recto, and V. W. Ruttan, "Price and Market Relationships for Rice and Corn in the Philippines," *Journal of Farm Economics*, vol. 48, no. 3, part I (August, 1966), pp. 685–703, where an examination of the behavior of the margin between the retail price and the farm price when the retail price fluctuates suggests that arbitrary market power of traders is found only in a few isolated areas. See also P. T. Bauer and B. S. Yamey, "Competition and Prices: A Study of Groundnut Buying in Nigeria," *Economica*, new series, vol. 19, no. 73 (February, 1952), pp. 31–43.

economically justified. If the returns will cover costs including risk cost, entrepreneurs will undertake the project; if the returns will not cover costs, the project will not represent an efficient allocation of resources.[23]

Second, take the case in which entrepreneurs overestimate the risk. Economically desirable ventures may then not be carried out, and government intervention may be appropriate. The failing, however, is not inherent in private enterprise but is traceable to a possible defect in a society's entrepreneurship. The proper form of government intervention, therefore, is not necessarily the establishment of public enterprises; an alternative, and perhaps superior, approach is to improve the quality of entrepreneurship, if possible.

Third, take the case in which excessive timidity or conservatism on the part of entrepreneurs makes them either demand an exorbitant price for undertaking highly risky ventures or, at the extreme, refuse to undertake a particular venture at any price. Willingness to take risk is the essential function of entrepreneurship. What this case illustrates is a shortage of entrepreneurship. Public policy may be directed toward increasing the supply of entrepreneurship through either an increase in public entrepreneurs (in public enterprises) or the development of private entrepreneurs.

Great size as an obstacle to a private economic undertaking is essentially a problem of raising funds; for, given access to the requisite funds, private entrepreneurs will not find size a greater obstacle than will government. If the project is economically sound, the inability to obtain the funds for it, whatever its size, must be the result of a defective capital-funds market.[24] Public policy may then seek a solution either through public enterprise or through the improvement of the funds market.

---

[23] I am abstracting here from conditions, discussed already, which would justify projects that will not cover costs.

[24] This difficulty should not be confused with the entirely different question of whether saving is great enough to permit the desired investment.

the distribution of income

The economic case for government modification of the distribution of income rests on the proposition of welfare economics that a redistribution of income toward greater equality is likely to add more to the total satisfaction of the recipients than it deducts from that of the losers, thus increasing the aggregate satisfaction of the society. This proposition cannot be rigorously demonstrated, since the satisfaction gained and lost cannot be measured and compared. There is, nevertheless, a presumption that when income distribution is highly unequal, the marginal satisfaction (the satisfaction yielded by the last unit of income) is less for people with high incomes than for people with low incomes. Moreover, there is some reason to believe that the loss of satisfaction incurred by the upper-income households through a redistribution of income is partially offset by a gain in their satisfaction from improving the well-being of the poorer members of their society. Voluntary contributions are a demonstration of the existence of such a gain.

The case for some degree of redistribution of income toward equality is generally accepted, but the guidelines for determining the degree are blurred. Plainly, complete equalization of income is not the way to maximize welfare. One reason is that income differences themselves perform certain equalizing functions. Incomes that compensate for effort, risk, unpleasant conditions, or investment in training tend to equalize the total well-being of individuals.

A second difficulty in deciding on an equalization policy is that equalization carried sufficiently far entails some sacrifice of aggregate income and its growth; the further it is carried, the more income must be sacrificed to move another degree toward equality. This is so, for one thing, because incomes serve as inducements to perform economic functions, and when the inducements are impaired, economic efficiency is reduced. In addition, the methods of redistributing income involve certain costs. Progressive taxation, which is probably the most efficient method, incurs increasing costs of enforcement and of uneconomic behavior arising from efforts by individuals to reduce their tax burden as the progressivity becomes steeper. Other policies which are intended to have an equalizing effect on income distribution, including price controls, the subsidizing of uneconomic enterprises, restrictions on trade and the movement of factors, have an even more drastic effect on aggregate income. At some point society must decide how much aggregate income it is willing to give up for greater equality of distribution.

A degree of equalization can be achieved along with an increase of aggregate income by policies which improve the functioning of the market system. Measures which reduce unemployment, increase the mobility of factors, and equalize educational and economic opportunities will both increase the efficiency of the economy and remove one of the causes of income inequality. In primarily agricultural countries where landownership is highly unequal and cultivation is done mainly by tenants, land reform is expected not only to reduce income inequality but also raise agricultural productivity by increasing farmers' incentives for improving their inputs and techniques. In general, the whole process of economic development automatically carries with it a major equalizing effect by spreading education, widening opportunities, and increasing the relative scarcity of labor and reducing the relative scarcity of property.

In a developed economy with a well-functioning market system, the case for substantial redistribution of income among the factors of production in the market does not appear to be strong. The serious need for redistribution is among those who are partially or wholly excluded from the market—the aged, the disabled, and the female heads of households. The poverty of such handicapped people can be alleviated only by direct assistance through income transfers.

decreasing-cost industries

One of the thorniest issues in the analysis of resource allocation is the determination of price and output in industries having decreasing costs. A decreasing-cost industry is an industry in which for technical reasons input is not finely divisible, so that the enterprise must begin with a large quantity of that indivisible input. As output is increased, the cost per unit of output (average cost) decreases. The cost of an *additional* unit of output (marginal cost) is less than the average cost (which includes the average fixed cost of the indivisible input). If output were increased enough, production would eventually reach a range of increasing average cost; but the size of the market may be limited, so that production must remain within the zone of decreasing costs.

If a price for the product is set at a point where it covers total cost, the price will exceed the cost of producing an additional unit (the marginal cost); and as long as the buyer is willing to pay more than the marginal cost, production will be less than the optimum. On the other hand, if the price is set equal to the marginal cost, total cost will not be covered. The proposal has therefore been made that the price be set equal to marginal cost and that the government make up the difference between total receipts and total cost from its general revenue.[25]

Where the enterprise already exists, either because it is possible to charge a price that covers total cost or because there was a mistaken notion that a price could be charged at which total cost would be covered, a theoretical argument can be made for marginal-cost pricing combined with a government subsidy.[26]

The same proposal, however, has been made with respect to *prospective* projects for which it would not be possible to charge a price that would cover all costs. The argument in favor of investment in such projects is in terms of consumers' surplus. The price consumers pay reflects the utility of the

[25] For an extended discussion of this proposal, see Nancy D. Ruggles, "The Welfare Basis of the Marginal Cost Pricing Principle," *Review of Economic Studies*, vol. 17, no. 1 (1949–1950), pp. 29–46, and "Recent Developments in the Theory of Marginal Cost Pricing," *ibid.*, vol. 17, no. 2 (1949–1950), pp. 107–126; also Robert W. Harbeson, "A Critique of Marginal Cost Pricing," *Land Economics*, vol. 31, no. 1 (February, 1955), pp. 54–74.

[26] See, however, the articles cited in the previous footnote for persuasive reasons, both theoretical and practical, for doubting that the marginal-cost pricing principle can be relied on to increase aggregate welfare.

marginal unit they buy, but the pre-marginal units they buy have a higher utility for them; thus consumers receive a surplus in that they would be willing to pay more than they actually do for the quantity they buy. Through price discrimination—charging varying prices per unit so as to extract a greater revenue from the consumers for the total quantity they buy—total receipts might be made to cover total costs. If so, the total value to consumers is said to exceed the cost, and the project is economically justified. (Discriminatory prices will not, in fact, be charged; it is sufficient to the argument to show that discrimination *could* yield revenue at least equal to total cost.)

The consumers'-surplus argument for projects that cannot cover total cost contains a fundamental fallacy. The cost of the product is taken as a measure of the value to consumers of the alternative products which might have been bought instead. The valuation of these alternative products does not include any consumers' surplus. A comparison is thus being made between the value of one product including consumers' surplus and the value of other products excluding consumers' surplus. A correct comparison between the value of alternative products must be based on the same valuation procedure for all products; if consumers' surplus is to be included in the value of one, it must be included in the value of the alternatives. Unless *all* allocative decisions are to be based on calculations that include consumers' surplus (a procedure which is rendered impractical by the problem of measuring consumers' surplus), the principle is not applicable.

international transactions

Most of the economic arguments for government intervention in international transactions have their basis, if they have any basis at all, in the propositions already discussed. For example, international transactions involving instability, speculation, maldistribution of income, and divergence of private from social costs have been used, rightly or wrongly, as grounds for government controls over international exchange.

A distinctive argument for government intervention in international trade is the infant-industry argument for the restriction of imports. A country may have a potential industry which, once established and developed, will be able to survive without protection. During its developmental phase, however, the industry's costs might be too high to permit it to compete with imports. Restriction of imports is one method of assisting an infant industry to be established and to grow to self-supporting maturity. The argument is subject to abuse; it has been used to justify protection of industries which will never grow out of the need for protection. Even if the industry does develop to the point where it no longer needs protection, it may be that the gains from having established the industry will never compensate for the costs incurred during the period of protection. Nevertheless, some economically defensible examples are likely to be found in the newly developing countries.

marginal product of labor below subsistence wage

A special case of a market defect in a few densely populated countries in the early phases of development has attracted considerable attention. When the supply of labor is very large relative to the supply of other inputs, a portion of the labor force will have such low productivity that the value of its product will be below the subsistence wage. If the employer must pay the subsistence wage, such labor will not be hired. This underemployment can eventually be eliminated by the accumulation of capital, but in the meantime, because of the gap between the potential productivity of the excess labor and the lowest wage that can be paid, potential product of the unemployed labor is being lost. The unemployed individuals are, of course, receiving a subsistence income in some way, generally through their families. The normal operation of the market, however, cannot secure from them what they might otherwise contribute to total product. Government intervention may increase aggregate welfare by some technique which is equivalent to a tax on the more productive members of the economy to subsidize the employment of the less productive.

OPTIMIZING THE RATE OF SAVING

Increasing the rate of saving is one of the most generally recommended economic functions of government and, among the less developed countries, would probably be ranked as the most important. Yet the bases for this intervention, and the principles for determining the optimum saving policy, are still incompletely understood. The appendix to this chapter reviews the basic theory and some recent explorations of this subject. The following discussion summarizes only the main conclusions.

For each individual there can be presumed to be some plan for distributing his consumption over his lifetime so as to maximize his total satisfaction. The optimum amount for him to consume and to save in each period will be related to his expected future income stream and his expected future needs. It will also be related to the rate of return on saving, which measures the rate at which consumption can be increased in the future by postponing consumption now.

The government may intervene to compel individuals to save more in their earlier years so as to be able to consume more in their later years. The proposition that individual welfare will thereby be increased is based on two arguments: (1) Individuals may be irrational, in the sense that they do not save so much in their earlier years as their own calculations would show to be optimal; (2) The rate of return to saving may be greater than the rate which individuals use in their calculations. This discrepancy occurs if there are external returns to saving—benefits arising from saving which accrue to society rather than to the individual savers.

The welfare arguments for forced saving become more tenuous when the purpose is not to maximize the welfare of the savers during their lifetime, but to increase the potential consumption of succeeding generations. Where, in the absence of a compulsory-saving program, the succeeding generation would have a lower per capita income than the present, a

31

presumptive welfare argument can be made for compelling the present generation to save more in order to bequeath a larger capital stock. But where, as the analysis in the appendix to this chapter suggests, the succeeding generation is likely, in any event, to have a higher per capita income than the present generation, the argument becomes difficult to sustain.

appendix to chapter 2

THE OPTIMUM RATE OF SAVING

The analysis of optimal saving begins with the definition of an optimal-saving plan as seen from the point of view of an individual. Then the reasons why individuals may fail to fulfill their optimal plan and why the sum of the individual optimal plans may not yield a social optimum are examined.

Assume that the objective of the economy is to maximize the utility derived from consumption by individuals during their lifetime. The optimum-saving plan for each individual will then be one which, through saving in some periods and dissaving in others, distributes his consumption over his lifetime in a way that maximizes his total lifetime utility, leaving zero net saving at the end. Assume further that each individual knows the amount of income he will receive each year, the number of years he will live, and his "needs" (the utility of consumption) per year. His saving decisions will then depend upon (1) the rate at which his marginal utility from consumption diminishes as his consumption per year increases;[1] (2) the

---

[1] The assumption of diminishing marginal utility will be retained throughout this discussion since it seems the most reasonable one for the range of consumption choices available to most people. But Milton Friedman and L. J. Savage argue persuasively in "The Utility Analysis of Choices Involving Risk," *Journal of Political Economy*, vol. 61, no. 4 (August, 1948), pp. 279–304, that for large increases of consumption permitting the consumer to enter upon a new and quite different way of life, marginal utility may increase. Quite possibly, certain cases of "spendthrift" behavior—a period of high living followed by hard times —can be rationalized as a utility-maximizing choice under conditions of increasing marginal utility.

rate at which he can exchange present consumption for future consumption; (3) his *pure time preference*—a preference for present over future consumption, though it involves a lower marginal utility now and a sacrifice of a higher marginal utility in the future.

In the simplest case—where (1) the return (interest) earned by saving is zero, so that one unit of present consumption exchanges for one unit of future consumption; (2) pure time preference is zero; (3) the marginal-utility function is the same in all years; (4) the individual is certain of his income receipts and the length of his life—total utility will be maximized by consuming equal amounts in each year. This conclusion follows from the fact that, with the given assumptions, equal consumption in each year will mean equal utility derived from the marginal unit of consumption in each year. Unless marginal utility is equated in all years, total utility will not be maximized, for by shifting consumption from a year of lower marginal utility to a year of higher marginal utility, total utility can be increased. For the typical individual, whose income is higher in his working years than in his old age, utility will be maximized by saving (during his years of higher income) the income in excess of his annual average income and dissaving in old age the amount by which his income falls below his annual average.

Varying assumption number 1, we introduce a positive rate of interest on saving. One unit of present consumption can now be given up in exchange for more than one unit of consumption in the future. Total lifetime consumption can now be increased by saving. On the other hand, shifting consumption from the present to the future tends to raise the marginal utility of present consumption and to decrease the marginal utility of future consumption. The possibility of raising total lifetime utility by increasing saving, therefore, depends on the opposed effects of the rate at which total consumption can be raised by present saving, and the rate at which marginal utility diminishes as consumption per time period increases. With a given marginal-utility curve, the higher the rate of interest, the more utility can be gained by postponing consumption. The more rapidly marginal utility diminishes with rising consumption, the less the utility that can be gained by postponing consumption.

If we now drop assumption 2 and introduce a positive time preference, the individual's behavior will be modified by his preference for enjoying his consumption sooner rather than later, with the result that current saving will be reduced. The individual's optimum-saving pattern will be further modified if—dropping assumption 3—his utility function is scheduled to change over time. The utility of consumption may, for example, be expected to decline in old age, in which case saving in earlier years will be less, compared with the patterns derived from the assumption of an unchanging utility function.

Finally—dropping the certainty assumption, number 4—the individual may be uncertain about his future income, his future utility function, and the length of his life. If he bases his saving decisions on the most probable expectations, there is still some chance that he will save more than the optimal amount in his earlier years and dissave more than the optimal amount in his later years, with, perhaps, net saving left at the time of his death because of uncertainty about the length of his life. Conversely, there is some chance that he will save less than the optimum in his earlier years and be compelled to dissave less than the optimum in his later years. If the chances of overshooting and undershooting the optimum-saving target are equal and if the individual considers the loss of utility in both cases equal, uncertainty will have no effect on his saving pattern. However, if he considers the penalties of saving too little for his old age to be greater than the penalties of saving too much, the effect of uncertainty will be to cause him to save more than the optimum in the years in which he saves and to dissave less than the optimum in the years in which he dissaves.

The basis for government intervention in the determination of saving (given the objective of maximizing lifetime utility) must lie in some incapacity of the individual to carry out an optimal-saving program. Three possible defects in the saving decisions of individuals can be suggested.

1. The rate of return on saving which the individual uses for his calculation (the private rate) may be less than the total

rate of return (the social rate), which includes both the returns to the individual and the returns from his saving that accrue to the rest of society. Several examples of returns to saving which are not received by the individual saver can be cited. Part of the increment of product resulting from an increment of capital accrues to society through taxes. Another part may either be taken by a rise of the price of other inputs or be distributed to society through a fall in the price of output. Another type of return to saving which is external to the individual saver is the gain in national security or national prestige that society acquires from an expansion of the economy. (By the same token, the additional power or prestige of one nation results in a loss of utility in other nations. Saving motivated by a competitive race among nations for military power or prestige is likely, in the end, to be a waste.) The effect, when a portion of the return to saving is external to the saver, will obviously be to induce lower-than-optimal saving.[2]

2. To the extent that consumers have a pure time preference, their saving will be below the optimal. The exercise of time preference, by definition, represents a diminution of total utility, since it is defined as a shift in consumption from periods of higher to periods of lower marginal utility. It reflects a miscalculation, a failure of foresight or self-control, a defect in our "telescopic faculty" (in Pigou's phrase) or "the conquest of reason by passion" (in Harrod's).[3]

3. Uncertainty about future income, the future utility function, and the length of one's life will probably affect saving in a manner opposite to time preference. That is, for those who prefer oversaving in their earlier years to undersaving, uncertainty will counteract time preference. The consumer who meets uncertainty by consuming less than the most probable optimum consumption in his earlier years is risking a moderate loss of lifetime utility to protect himself against a catastrophic

[2] In the same way, external returns to labor will also occur, creating a case for government intervention to compel longer hours of work than would be voluntarily worked in response to the wage rate. This makes the argument a rather troublesome one in a free society.

[3] R. F. Harrod, *Towards a Dynamic Economics* (London: Macmillan & Co., Ltd., 1949), p. 40.

loss of utility in his old age, a choice which is analogous to buying insurance.

The external economies of saving and the existence of time preference (not fully offset by the effect of uncertainty) can create a case for a government compulsory-saving and old-age-benefit program. It is administratively impossible to gear the compulsory-saving pattern to the optimal requirements of each individual, even were they known. A program that will produce a closer approximation to the average optimal saving behavior is the best that can be hoped for. Individuals who find themselves moved further away from their optimum by the government program can attempt to correct this outcome by altering their private saving and dissaving schedules. There remains the possibility that the government effort to raise total utility by its saving program will be defeated by a general tendency to adjust private saving and dissaving to cancel out the compulsory saving. Social security programs are based on the presumption that consumers will not reduce private saving, thus offsetting the government's program and leaving their consumption paths unchanged through time.

The attempt to define an optimum-saving program has thus far included the assumption that the consumer will maximize his total utility by consuming his total lifetime income, leaving zero saving at his death. A problem which has been evaded must now be faced: What are the obligations of one generation to the next with regard to capital accumulation?

If each consuming unit saves in its earlier years and dissaves in its later years, ending with zero net assets, the nation's capital stock will nevertheless grow, provided population and income are growing.[4] That, however, is not the sole explanation for a growing capital stock. The consumer's plan for maximizing his utility frequently includes an *estate motive:*

[4] In a growing population the number of people in the saving age group will be increasing by more than the number in the dissaving age group. With rising wage rates, the income of savers (who are mostly employed) will be increasing by larger absolute amounts than the income of dissavers (most of whom are wholly or partially retired). Consequently saving will be increasing by greater absolute amounts than dissaving.

the desire to bequeath assets to family, friends, or worthy causes. There is no assurance that the heirs will not adopt a consumption level that will exhaust their inheritances by the end of their lives. Provided, however, they have an estate motive no weaker than their benefactors', the capital stock each generation bequeaths to the next will grow on this account.

Precisely what the capital-stock obligations are of one generation to the next is a vexing question. No clear basis has been established in welfare economics for rejecting the objective that each generation maximize its own welfare. But attempts have been made to show that the additional capital left by the present to the next generation is, in fact, less than the amount that would maximize the present generation's own welfare, when the decision is left entirely to individual choice. One recent line of analysis, by Stephen A. Marglin, argues that adding to the capital for future generations yields benefits to the present generation which are external to the individual and therefore do not enter into his calculations.[5] On the basis of these external benefits, a case is made for government intervention to increase saving.

The essential assumption in Marglin's analysis is that the individual derives an altruistic satisfaction from contributing to an increase in the standard of living of others. If his altruism motivates him to bequeath assets to the next generation, he has, in effect, a *social* estate motive. Presumably this motive is distinct from his desire to leave assets to his family or friends, a *private* estate motive sufficiently close to his personal interests as not to involve altruism.

The gist of Marglin's analysis is the following. A dollar saved and invested by the present generation will permit more consumption by the next generation. On the assumption that the next generation will feel obligated to pass on its received capital intact to its successor, the additional consumption will be equal to the marginal product of $1 of capital during the

[5] "The Social Rate of Discount and the Optimal Rate of Investment," *Quarterly Journal of Economics*, vol. 77, no. 1 (February, 1963), pp. 95–111. See also Amartya Kumar Sen, "On Optimising the Rate of Saving," *Economic Journal*, vol. 71, no. 283 (September, 1961), pp. 479–496.

lifetime of the generation that inherits it. We will call that amount k.

Let a represent the satisfaction or utility which a member of the present generation receives from contemplating the addition of \$1 of consumption to the next generation's total consumption. Then his utility derived from his altruistic sacrifice of \$1 of consumption will equal ak. His net gain of utility will be ak minus the loss of the utility of the \$1 of his own consumption. For simplification, assume that utility is measured on a scale such that \$1 of his own consumption has a utility of one. The individual will be motivated to leave capital to the next generation if ak is greater than one. Presumably, a will be less than one, and, except for unusually altruistic persons, we would expect it to be a rather small fraction. Hence, unless k has an extremely high value, it is improbable that altruism will lead to any saving.[6]

Now, suppose that the individual can vote on a proposal that he and each of his contemporaries leave an equal amount to the next generation. Assume the present and future generations each have n members. For each \$1 of consumption that the present generation sacrifices, the next generation will obtain a total increase of consumption of kn, and our individual in the present generation will derive utility equal to akn from contemplating the gain of the next generation. However, his altruism will also cause him to lose some utility from observing the sacrifice of his contemporaries. Let b represent the deduction from his utility because of the sacrifice of \$1 of consumption by his contemporaries. His total loss of utility on that account will be $b(n-1)$. The balance of his gains and losses (including the loss of utility, equal to one, from his own sacrifice of \$1 of consumption) will be

$$akn - b(n-1) - 1$$

and the individual will gain from the community-saving proposal if this expression is positive.

[6] For example, assume that from adding to the consumption of the next generation one derives as much as one-tenth of the satisfaction he derives from consuming that amount himself. Then k would have to exceed ten in order for altruism to motivate saving. Unfortunately, capital is rarely, if ever, that productive.

If n is large, the relative significance of the "-1," representing the loss of utility through the sacrifice of the individual's own consumption, becomes trivial. For a large n, therefore, the condition under which the individual will gain from the community-saving proposal approaches the requirement that ak be greater than b. That condition may well exist. If it does, society, if presented with a proposal for collective saving to provide a higher level of income for the next generation, will choose to save more than if they had made all saving decisions separately.[7]

The Marglin analysis is intended to establish only the possibility that individuals, participating in a joint plan to increase the capital stock to be left to the future, might choose to leave more than the sum of the separate bequests they would severally make; and that, through voting procedure, their choice of the optimal amount of joint saving could be determined. (In a non-democracy, the decision would have to depend on the authorities' own preferences or on their estimates of the public's preference.)

The significance of this proposition, in terms of the amount of saving involved, is unknown. The coefficients a and b are taken as constant for small changes in the amount deducted from present consumption to be left to the future. However, as the amount is increased, a will decrease and b will increase. The brighter the future prospects look and the more the present is deprived, the less utility we gain from bequeathing to the future and the more utility we lose from seeing our contemporaries deprived. Should the values of a and b change rapidly, the point where ak equals b might be reached at quite small amounts of joint saving.[8]

A similar limitation results from the tendency for k to fall as the capital stock grows. The productivity of capital declines as

[7] The collective provision for posterity may, of course, reduce the motivation for private bequests to posterity, so that the net change of saving will be less than anticipated.

[8] Gordon Tullock has argued that it is highly improbable that ak is greater than b, even at zero joint saving. In an economy with technological progress and the usual individual propensity to save, it can be expected that the next generation will have a higher per capita income than the present generation without a program of joint saving. It does

capital accumulates, unless this tendency is offset by increases in labor input or innovations. Given the rate of labor increase and the rate of technological discovery, an increase in the rate of capital accumulation reduces the rate at which present sacrifices of consumption can contribute to future consumption, and thus limits the level of joint saving which altruism will motivate.

An ingenious proposition suggesting a simple resolution of any apparent conflict between generations over the rate of investment has recently been provided by growth theorists.[9] The long-run equilibrium growth rate, as has been shown,[10] depends on the rate of technological progress and the rate of growth of labor input, and is independent of the rate of saving, given the assumption that technological progress and labor growth are independent of the rate of saving. The long-run growth rate is thus given, but the path along which growth proceeds may be higher or lower depending on the capital-output ratio. That is, by increasing the saving ratio, capital can be made to grow faster than output, and the economy can grow faster during a transitional phase, but eventually the capital-output ratio reaches a new equilibrium, and the growth rate (which declines throughout the transitional phase) is once again equal to the original long-run or "natural" growth rate.

On the assumption that the natural growth rate is determined and the society has the choice only of which path to be

---

not seem likely that an individual will gain satisfaction by depriving his generation in order to increase the wealth of the succeeding generation, which, in any event, will be wealthier than his own. "The Social Rate of Discount and the Optimal Rate of Investment: Comment," *Quarterly Journal of Economics,* vol. 78, no. 2 (May, 1964), pp. 331–336.

[9] Edmund Phelps, "The Golden Rule of Accumulation," *American Economic Review,* vol. 51, no. 4 (September, 1961), pp. 638–643; Joan Robinson, "A Neo-classical Theorem," *Review of Economic Studies,* vol. 29 (3), no. 80 (June, 1962), pp. 219–226.

[10] T. W. Swan, "Economic Growth and Capital Accumulation," *Economic Record,* vol. 32, no. 63 (November, 1956), pp. 334–361; Robert M. Solow, "A Contribution to the Theory of Economic Growth," *Quarterly Journal of Economics,* vol. 70, no. 1 (February, 1956), pp. 65–94.

on, it can be shown that there is only one path, and therefore only one rate of saving, which maximizes consumption for each generation. Moreover, the rate of saving that maximizes consumption is the same for each generation. Hence each generation, in seeking to maximize its own consumption, is choosing the rate of saving which the next generation would like to choose for itself. If the problem is simplified by assuming that one rate of saving is to be chosen for all time, one rate of saving that will satisfy all generations can be chosen.

In a *golden age,* with income growing at the natural rate and the capital-output ratio brought to the point that maximizes consumption, altruism as a ground for altering the saving ratio washes out. Nothing is to be gained by saving more for the next generation if the next generation will be obligated to do the same for its successors. Consumption will be reduced for all generations by choosing a saving ratio greater than the optimum. The best that can be done in the golden age is for each generation to choose the saving ratio that maximizes its own consumption.

But a decision about the transitional phase remains to be made. If the economy is off the golden-age growth path, the question is how quickly society wishes to get on it—that is, how much to raise or lower the rate of saving until the capital-output ratio is adjusted to the optimum level and the rate of saving can be set at the golden-age rate. The altruism argument might play a part in this decision, leading society to choose to shorten the transitional period.

The golden-age analysis does not provide precise practical answers, but it is highly suggestive. What it chiefly suggests is that in countries which have enjoyed long-term growth and in which individuals' gains from saving do not diverge much from the social gains, the capital-output ratio and the saving ratio are likely to be close to the optimum. The need for government saving or dissaving to maintain the optimum capital stock over the long run (not to be confused with short-run government saving or dissaving for anti-fluctuations purposes) will, in that case, be quite small. The case of the relatively undeveloped economies, where different initial conditions prevail, will be taken up in Chapter 6.

3 | planning—a word
in search of a meaning

Anyone who reads in the extensive literature on economic planning encounters early and often the proposition that "planning" is normal, unavoidable, ubiquitous. "The prudent housewife prepares her shopping list before setting out to the shops. What is this but planning and control?" [1] "The American Telephone and Telegraph Company plans. The Ford Motor Company plans. The railroads have realized the same necessity and plan for tomorrow. Are we to believe planning is wise everywhere except in the commonwealth itself?" [2]

Obviously this use of the term "planning" is so general as to be meaningless. Many other applications of the word are in use to compound the confusion. When I consider what to do with the word, I am strongly tempted by Frank Lloyd Wright's advice as consultant on the redevelopment of Pittsburgh: "Abandon it." But "planning" is now a word too widely used to be dismissed. It will have to be rehabilitated. As Dahl and Lindblom put it,

[1] Sir Oliver Franks, *Central Planning and Control in War and Peace* (Cambridge, Mass.: Harvard University Press,1947), p. 25.

[2] Albert Lauterbach, *Economic Security and Individual Freedom* (Ithaca, N.Y.: Cornell University Press, 1948), p. 63, quoting from Bishop Bromley Oxnam.

A good purpose is to be served by reclaiming a useful concept such as planning from the fires of sterile controversy. Whether one likes it or not, words are sometimes the masters of men; and no small part of the barrenness of the controversy over planning is due to man's confusion of the attempt to be rational with the forms the attempts sometimes take simply because the word "planning" has been used to describe both. If the word is rehabilitated, so also is the analysis of the process. The gain is not merely terminological.[3]

Recent efforts to make "planning" a useful word have fallen sadly short of their mark. Dahl and Lindblom, for example, offer the definition, ". . . planning is an attempt at rationally calculated action to achieve a goal." [4] All the rest of their planning discussion comes down to the *forms* of the attempts at rationally calculated action. The Dahl-Lindblom solution to the reclamation problem is essentially the same as Wright's Pittsburgh solution. If "planning" is used only to mean attempts at rationally calculated action as distinguished from attempts at irrationally calculated or uncalculated action, the term is made superfluous, and, for all practical purposes, has been abandoned.[5]

---

[3] Robert A. Dahl and Charles E. Lindblom, *Politics, Economics, and Welfare* (New York: Harper & Brothers, 1953), pp. 20–21.

[4] *Ibid.*, p. 20.

[5] A similar approach is proposed by John E. Elliott, "Economic Planning Reconsidered," *Quarterly Journal of Economics,* vol. 72, no. 1 (February, 1958), pp. 55–76. Economic planning "connotes one general characteristic, viz., the attempt to apply reason and foresight to the ordering of human affairs and the attainment of human purposes [p. 56]." Under that broad and useless umbrella, he then lists various "types of economic planning," in pursuit of the question of what planning really is.

There is nothing wrong with this approach except that it makes the term unnecessary. If "economic planning" is to serve only the function of narrowing the discussion of economic organization to the field of attempts to apply reason and foresight in economic affairs, it becomes redundant, since economic organization presumes reason and foresight.

A PRECISE DEFINITION OF "PLANNING"

The controversy raging around the subject of economic planning, while not so barren as Dahl and Lindblom suggest, has certainly been confused, largely because the participants have not agreed on, and frequently have not known, exactly what "planning" means. The damage has not been purely intellectual. Economic policies have shared the confusion, with costly results, as I shall subsequently undertake to illustrate.

I believe it is possible to give "economic planning" a precise meaning which will illuminate the critical issues and sharpen the distinctions between opposed positions. The roots of the notion of planning are to be found in the proposition that when decisions are made at a decentralized level where the decision maker knows about or is concerned with only a part of the total process, the optimal decisions cannot be made. The individual unit allocates resources on the basis of the costs and benefits which accrue to that unit. From the social viewpoint, the relevant data for the allocation of resources are the costs and benefits which accrue to the whole society, which, in certain instances, may differ from (be more inclusive than) the data that concern the individual unit. *Planning is the attempt, by centralizing the management of the allocation of resources sufficiently, to take into account social costs and social benefits which would be irrelevant to the calculations of the decentralized decision maker.*[6]

This definition of planning may be criticized as being less precise than it appears to be on first examination. The level of decision making rises with the scale of the management unit.

[6] The only clear statement of this essential element in the definition of planning that I have found in the economic-planning literature is in E. F. M. Durbin, *Problems of Economic Planning* (London: Routledge & Kegan Paul, Ltd., 1949), p. 44: "The element common to all the forms of new control we regard as 'Planning' is the extension of the size of the unit of management and the consequent enlargement of the field surveyed when any economic decision is taken."

Larger firms can take into account more data than smaller firms, an industry under one management more than a segment of the industry, several industries merged under one management more than one industry, and so on. Is there, then, no clear distinction between planning and non-planning, but only a continuous line of ascent from less planning to more planning? The clear distinction is provided by the critical difference between the basis for decisions of private management of any size and the basis for the decisions of government. The interests, resources, and powers of the private unit, no matter how large, are limited in a way which distinguishes, not only in degree but in kind, its decision making from the decision making which is possible for the government. Planning, therefore, is an effort by the *government* to improve the allocation of resources by the use of cost and benefit data calculated from the viewpoint of the whole society.

Planning is a government activity, but not all government activity is planning. A government may, for example, direct economic activity on the basis of the same calculations that a private enterprise would use. It may use even less complete calculations than a private enterprise would use. The government is attempting to plan only when it undertakes to improve economic allocation by introducing into the calculations elements which it would be improbable or impossible for a private enterprise to introduce.

The occasion for planning arises, therefore, from some ineradicable defects in the process of making decisions at the private-enterprise level. The decentralized private-enterprise system relies for its coordination on the market mechanism, which may be over-briefly described as a system where individuals, given their preferences and objectives, decide on the purchase and sale of inputs and outputs on the basis of relative prices, and those prices, being free to change in response to individual transactions in the market, act as signals of preferences and of the relative scarcity of inputs and outputs. The alleged ineradicable defects in the decentralized private-enterprise arrangement consist, therefore, of certain shortcomings of prices in controlling the flow of inputs and outputs.

I surveyed in Chapter 2 the grounds for government intervention in a basically private-enterprise economy. Government interventions pursued on certain of these grounds are planning activities. Specifically, those government economic policies are planning activities which represent efforts to improve economic decisions by substituting calculations based on social data for private calculations which would omit relevant data. Let me cull from Chapter 2 the market defects which create a case for planning.

1 Situations in which there are non-market interdependencies or externalities.

2 Situations in which the prices that emerge from the market process are false signals, in that they do not correctly reflect (a) what the additional production of one commodity will cost in terms of foregone production of other commodities and (b) the rate at which buyers are willing to give up each product to obtain more of each alternative product. These cases include price distortions because of imperfect competition, decreasing-cost industries, and underemployment of labor because its marginal product is below the subsistence wage.

3 Situations in which the response of decision makers to correct information is chronically irrational and leads to a social outcome which is less than optimal. Household decisions with respect to saving and producers' exaggeration of investment risks are possible examples.

WHAT PLANNING IS NOT

So common and confusing has become the practice of referring to all government economic activity as "planning" that it is important, for the sake of clarity, to go beyond defining what planning is and to explain what it is not.

Government operation of enterprises is not per se planning. The enterprises may be operated on the same principles and guidelines as private enterprises.

The variety of government activities devoted to improving the operation of the market is obviously not planning but its direct opposite. Included here are regulations to reduce monopoly power or to limit the exercise of monopoly power so as to bring the results of the market closer to the optimum. Also included are programs to increase the mobility of the factors of production. Finally, efforts to increase the supply of information to individual decision-making units are, in a market-operated economy, not planning, but attempts to improve the working of the market.

In this category of government intervention to improve the operation of the market are included two major types of public program which are frequently labeled "planning." The first of these is *stabilization:* the use of monetary and fiscal policies to adjust aggregate demand when it threatens to become either excessive or insufficient relative to the attainable levels of total production.

When there is unemployment, the market is subject to a major source of error arising from divergence between the labor costs on which producers base their decisions and the social costs of labor. The alternative cost of unemployed labor to society is zero, while the price of labor is necessarily greater than zero. When the government intervenes to bring about full employment, it is, in effect, improving the functioning of the market by bringing toward equality the market cost and the social cost of inputs. In a pure stabilization program, one not mixed with other objectives, choices are left to individual, decentralized decision makers. Similarly, in eliminating excess demand, the government is undertaking to remove an impediment to the efficient functioning of the price mechanism, improving rather than supplementing the decentralized decision-making process.

The exclusion of stabilization from the planning sphere is more than a terminological quibble. The inadequacy of the self-stabilizing mechanisms in the economic system is unquestionably an instance of failure of the market economy; but the nature of the corrective measures required is quite different from what is required in other cases of market failures like those arising from externalities. The stabilization correctives strengthen the market mechanism, while the externalities problem calls for methods of decision making that replace the market mechanism. This important distinction can be kept in sight by reserving the term "planning" for the latter policies and denying it to the former.

A second major area of government economic effort which is commonly and loosely called "planning" is *forecasting*. Virtually all decision making involves an element of forecasting. In making any choice which can be postponed, some type of forecast is involved, explicitly or implicitly, in order to decide on the best timing. Whenever the wisdom of a choice depends to some extent on future conditions, choosing implies forecasting. Forecasting, therefore, is an integral part of decentralized private decision making.

Government forecasting in the context of a decentralized market economy is an effort to improve the functioning of the market by contributing to the improvement of the forecasts used by the members of the market. It is not planning.

Government forecasting as an aid to government decisions represents no fundamental departure from the method of private, decentralized decision making, which, as has been pointed out, also requires forecasts. The fact that it is government forecasting for government decisions does not make it planning in any sense distinguishable from the private decentralized method.

The function of government in the area of forecasting, aside from improving its own decisions, is to improve the operation of the market by increasing the range of information available to private decision makers. The capacity of the government to perform this function depends, of course, on its ability to increase the knowledge about the future, an ability which still remains to be demonstrated.

The prevailing view of the relation between forecasting and planning represents a basic confusion. Planning, rather than increasing the use of forecasting, is a method intended to reduce the need for forecasting. In a decentralized (nonplanning) system, the individual decision maker must, in effect, forecast what other decision makers will do. Planning, which consists of a reduction in the number of decision makers by centralization of control, reduces the range of events that must be forecast.[7] The situation is much like a football game. Each player, to choose his own course, must forecast what his opponents will do and what each of his teammates will do. A team, by signals and by prearranged principles of action, improves the predictability for each player of his teammates' behavior. But a team might undertake to subordinate all its decisions to a central authority, which would eliminate part of the forecasting task, though leaving the need to forecast the behavior of the opponents.

The distinction between forecasting and planning is implicit in Scitovsky's concept of external economies when the investment decisions of firms or industries are interdependent.[8] If two industries are interdependent, so that the optimum rate of expansion in each is dependent on the rate of expansion in the other, decentralized decision making requires that each industry forecast the behavior of the other. With the aid of information regularly available to both parties and through exchanges of information and signals, reasonably accurate forecasts are possible. Like the members of a football team, independent

[7] To Maurice Dobb, this is the essential function of planning. "Instead of the allocation-pattern of investment being a product in the first instance of the guesses and expectations of a large number of independent decision-makers (*entrepreneurs*), in the long run 'revised' by *ex post* movements of market prices, economic planning essentially consists of an attempt to secure a co-ordinated set of investment decisions *ex ante* —in advance of any commitment of resources to particular constructional projects or installations." *An Essay on Economic Growth and Planning* (London: Routledge & Kegan Paul, Ltd., 1960), p. 5.

"At the core of the difference in this respect of which we have spoken between a planned and an atomistic market economy lies the factor of uncertainty. But it is an uncertainty of a special kind. If each decision-taker in a market economy could estimate future prices on the basis of present prices (which we have seen he cannot do) or if he could correctly estimate the investment-decisions being concurrently made by all other *entrepreneurs* throughout the system, and also those to be made at all future dates throughout the life-period of the concrete investment-project in question, the difference in question between the two economic mechanisms would disappear (with a qualification that we shall mention in a moment)." *Ibid.*, p. 7. (The qualification pertains to pure external economies.)

[8] See pp. 17–18 above.

firms and industries in a market can achieve remarkable coordination. The alternative arrangement, centralized decision making (planning), is a substitute for forecasting.

The uncertainty of producers about the decisions of other producers, which arises from incomplete exchange of information, has been called *secondary uncertainty.*[9] *Primary uncertainty* is the uncertainty which confronts producers from all other sources, including changes in consumer preferences, changes in the labor supply, technical discovery, and the behavior of "nature." Secondary uncertainty can be eliminated by the complete centralization of producers' decisions. However, if the centralized control extends only to national producers, then the decisions of foreign producers become part of the primary uncertainty. That source of uncertainty can be eradicated only by worldwide planning or by isolating the economy from the international economy.

ECONOMIC ORGANIZATION AND PLANNING

Planning is associated, in many minds, with a particular form of economic organization. However, in the sense in which I have defined it, planning can be visualized in a variety of economic settings. Four organizational choices are especially basic and significant: price versus non-price systems, private versus public ownership of enterprise, centralized versus decentralized calculation, and total versus partial planning.

price versus non-price systems

A system of planning in which decisions are controlled entirely through price signals is at least conceptually possible. The prices, however, would not in all cases be determined in the market. Since the case for planning originates in the instances of failure of prices to emit correct signals, planning would employ the price mechanism by attempting to correct market prices where necessary. A system of taxes and subsidies would

[9] See M. Dobb, *op. cit.,* p. 8. The terminology "primary" and "secondary" uncertainty is from Tjalling C. Koopmans, *Three Essays on the State of Economic Science* (New York: McGraw-Hill Book Company, 1957).

be applied—taxes to increase the prices of those items which are produced under conditions of external diseconomies, subsidies to lower the prices of items involving external economies or decreasing costs. Where the aim of planning is to reduce secondary uncertainty by centralizing decisions, taxes and subsidies would be used to expand or contract production to correct for the discrepancy between desired allocation as seen by the independent producing units and as seen by the Planning Commission.[10]

A non-price system of planning would require direct controls on economic activity by means of orders from the Planning Commission. All choices would be made at the planning level.

Price and non-price systems can be combined. A predominantly price-directed economy might apply direct planning controls in specific instances, such as zoning regulations to control land use; or in an economy in which production decisions are centrally determined, prices may be used to ration final output among consumers.

The possibility of planning while relying predominantly on the price mechanism has been questioned.[11] The actual objections, however, have their basis not in the impossibility of the combination but in doubts about the administrative efficiency of price signals compared to direct orders for transmitting the planner's information.[12] But the possibility of a form of organization and its relative efficiency are quite different ques-

[10] It may not be clear why this type of taxing and subsidizing should not be called "improving the market" rather than "planning." This policy is one in which the government intervenes to set a centrally calculated price. Market improvement seeks to improve the mechanism of the market, but it is still the *market* which determines the price.

[11] See, for example, Maurice Dobb, "A Note on Saving and Investment in a Socialist Economy," *Economic Journal,* vol. 49, no. 196 (December, 1939), pp. 713–728.

[12] For example, on the subject of using taxes for stabilization when investment is determined by decentralized decisions, Dobb notes that it can be done but says, "But it may well seem to many a somewhat strange 'Heath Robinson' mechanism to have to create a specialised device of variable social dividends or taxes in order to 'neutralise' money sufficiently for a system of accounting-prices to operate smoothly. . . ." *Ibid.,* pp. 723–724.

tions. On the question of the relative efficiency of a price system and central direction, there is much that will have to be said at a more appropriate point.

private versus public ownership

Public ownership of productive enterprises has no necessary connection with central planning. A system of public enterprises can operate in a wholly decentralized way, coordinated by a market-price system which simulates a private-enterprise market system. Conversely, central planning in a private-enterprise system is possible. The simplest method may be to manipulate prices through taxes and subsidies to bring about the planned allocation of resources, but direct controls on inputs and outputs are also possible. In saying that these forms are possible, I do not mean to imply anything about the potential efficiency of the effort to have public enterprises simulate private firms or to make private firms conform to a central plan.

centralized versus decentralized planning

Planning by definition implies some degree of central control, but the degree to which decision making may be decentralized varies widely. The extent of decentralization comes down, once again, to the extent of reliance on a price system. Without prices, coordinated decisions require complete centralization. The greater the scope given to the price mechanism, the more decentralization of decisions is possible.

total versus partial planning

Planning may be restricted to portions of the economic process in which the failures of a decentralized price system are of serious consequence, while the remainder of the economy, in which the price system is deemed to be operating satisfactorily, is omitted from the planning schemes. On the other hand, the interdependence of all economic decisions, however remote or trivial the connection, provides an argument for total planning for those who care to avail themselves of it.

SUMMARY

Intelligent discussion of the role of government in the economy has been obstructed by terminological confusion, particularly with respect to the word "planning." This word can be made useful by restricting it to a specific type of government economic activity, to wit: the attempt to allocate resources on the basis of calculations which reflect social costs and benefits in situations where those calculations diverge from the costs and benefits relevant to decentralized decision making.

Most varieties of government economic activity cannot be called "planning." In particular it should be noted that stabilization policies and forecasting, generally considered the kingpins of planning in the looser usages of the term, are in fact the direct opposite of planning. Their purpose is to improve the functioning of decentralized decision making.

Planning is not tied to any specific form of economic organization. It may be applied with or without the price mechanism, in a system of either private or public ownership of productive property; it may be centralized or decentralized; it may be partial or total.

4 | government in the economy: portrait with warts

The picture of the private-enterprise economy has been on the easel since Adam Smith's time, as successive generations of economists have painted in the details, missing none of the warts and blemishes, like those described in Chapter 3. On the other hand, the economists' portrait of government in the economy is a comparatively new work which is still in a state of classical idealization.

It is interesting to speculate on the reasons why economists have not brought to their portrait of government the same effort at realism we find in their portrait of the private economy. No doubt part of the explanation is that it is private enterprise that has predominated during the period in which economics has existed as a formal discipline, while opportunities to observe extensive government intervention have been limited until comparatively recent times. A second contributory cause has been the lag in the development of a science of government and public administration to match the rigorous economic theory of the private economy. Hence, when defects in the private economy could be demonstrated by theoretical analysis to be inherent in the decision-making process, the shortcomings of government in the economy have been regarded as superficial faults of execution, correctable by polishing up the machinery of administration.

Unquestionably, there has been increasing suspicion among economic theorists, fostered by the experience of recent years, that calling in the government to redress the balance of the private economy does not assure an improvement in economic management. But much analytical work remains to be done to demonstrate that certain major deficiencies of government in the economy are ineradicable and not merely examples of malpractice.

THE RULES OF THE PRIVATE GAME

The analysis of the functioning of a private economy rests upon certain rules which constitute the framework within which (it is assumed) the game will be played. The contrasting set of rules under which the government plays the economic game can be grasped most easily if we first review the private frame.

1 *Objectives of Decision Makers*
The objective of each decision maker is to maximize his welfare—by maximizing his expected return, in the case of the producer; by exchanging his productive service at the most advantageous terms, in the case of the seller of factor services; by maximizing his satisfaction, in the case of the consumer.

2 *The Test of Performance*
The test of the correctness of decisions and of efficiency is the reward to the decision maker. In particular, profits are the criterion for judging the soundness of decisions about investment and innovation and the efficiency of the management of an enterprise.

3 *The Correction of Poor Performance*
The tests which reveal poor performance act at the same time to eliminate it. Low profits or losses are the punishment for inefficiency and tend, eventually, to drive the inefficient out of the decision-making positions.

It is obvious that these rules of the private game are not absolute, but rather are a matter of degree. Economists have noted the possibility that objectives other than maximization of profits, such as the pursuit of security or "the quiet life," may motivate producers. Application of the test of performance and punishment for poor performance may, in some instances, be long delayed. Nevertheless, in private-enterprise economies, these rules predominate, and the exceptions are limited.

One can go further and say that the exceptions to these rules will be trivial, provided that *competition* is prevalent in the economy. Where competition operates, producers who neglect the pursuit of profits are eliminated because the test of performance is constantly being applied, and retribution is swift. The reasons for believing that competition can be adequate for the fulfillment of this function in any economy have been given in Chapter 2 (pp. 10 to 14).

THE PUBLIC WARTS

In Chapter 2, I reviewed the inherent characteristics of a decentralized private-enterprise economy which preclude its attaining an optimal performance. Here I examine the parallel case: the inherent characteristics of the public economy which preclude its attaining an optimum. From this discussion I exclude pseudo-public enterprises, that is, publicly owned enterprises constituted to reproduce exactly private enterprises, with the objectives of private enterprise: profits as the long-run test of performance, independent managers, and culling of managers or firms that fail the test. There are a number of enterprises that closely approximate these conditions (like the Renault automobile company in France), generally having arisen out of peculiar historical circumstances or an acute deficiency of private initiative. They are rare, however, for a variety of reasons. The most obvious is that, since they are replicas of private enterprise, there is ordinarily no point to substituting them for private enterprise. A second reason is that, since any enterprise must ultimately be responsible to its owners, it is extremely difficult for a government enterprise to obtain and maintain its independence.

Where government operation in the economy is of a genuinely public character and not private enterprise in disguise, it will face certain obstacles to ideal performance.

the clash of objectives

The image of government policy held by its more enthusiastic proponents is of the formulation of policy by "experts" to achieve well-defined ends which will maximize social welfare. Such a combination of ends is supposedly shown scientifically to be superior to any other combination, and the policy is then implemented. Except for some of the simpler policies (for example, compulsory smallpox inoculation), where substantial unanimity on ends prevails, this image is remote from reality. In general, disagreement about ends prevails; this makes the ideal policy ambiguous, and its adoption (even if it can be objectively determined) improbable.

As an illustration, consider the agricultural problem and policies as they exist in a number of developed countries. Among qualified students of the subject there is little disagreement on the nature and origins of the problem. The productivity of farmers has been rising faster than the demand for their product, with the result that farmers' prices and incomes tend to be depressed relative to the rest of the economy. In addition, some farmers using poor land and backward techniques have had little share in the general rise of productivity.

Economists agree on the broad outlines of the corrective policy that will maximize social welfare. Labor and other factors of production should be diverted from agriculture to more productive activity, a move which will both raise the total national product and correct the depressed conditions of the agricultural sector. This solution is precisely the one which the free market tends to bring about. The market's failure is solely its *speed* of adjustment—the movement of people out of farming, while large, has not been able to keep up with the rise of farm productivity—and the appropriate government policy would appear to be one which accelerates the market adjustment by facilitating the switch of farm population to other occupations. Yet this is precisely the policy which has not been pursued. Prices have been supported, surplus products stored or destroyed, quotas imposed on production; but no effort has been made to expedite the transfer of labor and capital being wasted in agriculture into productive uses. Indeed, one consequence of these policies is to keep and even attract resources into agriculture.

Even viewed as a palliative intended to support agricultural income until the market completes its adjustment, the prevailing agricultural policy does not come close to the ideal, or even to the intelligent. Price supports benefit the farmer in proportion to his production: The bulk of the additional income accrues to the highly productive units, while the less productive units, where the serious deprivation exists, receive the least.

If we inquire why society produces such an inferior policy, we find the explanation in the conflict of objectives. There are the regional business interests whose objective is to keep their market amongst the farmers. There are the political interests whose power would decline with the decline of agricultural population. There are the representatives of labor who fear an increase of competition if farmers are brought into industrial production. And there are the farmers who seek relief from maladjustment without making any adjustment.

The policy that finally emerges when society lacks a consensus on objectives is the product of a bargaining process. Except under special conditions governing the relative bargaining powers of the parties and involving a considerable element of chance, bargaining will not yield an optimal policy.

The settlement of conflicts of interest by bargaining is, basically, the democratic political process. The way to keep "politics" out of economic decisions might appear to be to dispense with democracy. A dictatorship, it will be said, having no need to bargain, can proceed directly to institute the optimal policy as determined by disinterested expert analysts. To anyone who includes democratic process as one of the essential ingredients of an optimal solution, the impossibility of optimality needs no further demonstration. We can go further, however, and note that the idea of dictatorship as a system in which all conflicts of interest are settled without compromise by a single arbiter who seeks to maximize social welfare has no basis in reality. The dictator may, in fact, not seek to maximize social welfare. Even if he does, he governs through a bureaucracy of officials with objectives of their own. An organization the size of a national government cannot avoid, without degenerating into chaos, the creation of a set of administrators with some independence in decision making and substantial influence through their control of information and their knowledge of the operations of their departments.[1] The policy that finally materializes is determined by the interplay of the various interest groups.[2]

---

[1] Between democracy and absolute dictatorship lies a zone in which the government is maintained by a more or less precarious balance of military, regional, economic, and other interests. The more precarious the balance, the more difficult the government finds it to approach the rational economic solution of the experts.

[2] "While safeguarding his own personal domination against any possibility of challenge, Stalin was compelled to give his authority institutional expression. The great bureaucratic hierarchies of the Party, the secret police, the armed forces, state administration, and industrial management remained subject to his direction, but they also operated as centers of influence in their own right. Each of them represented a pool of functional competence on which Stalin had to draw in order to effect his purposes. Individuals might be, and were, expendable, but the apparatus as a whole was indispensable. Each of its specialized parts manifested the characteristics of bureaucracy everywhere. Each arm of the apparatus viewed decisions from the vantage point of its own particular interests, and it struggled to defend and expand the area of its own domination. Behind the monolithic facade of Stalinist totalitarianism, the plural pressures of professional bureaucratic interests found expression." Merle Fainsod, *How Russia Is Ruled,* rev. ed. (Cambridge, Mass.: Harvard University Press, 1963), p. 579.

See also Barrington Moore, Jr., *Soviet Politics: The Dilemma of Power* (Cambridge, Mass.: Harvard University Press, 1950), especially "Policy Execution and the Vested Interest in Confusion," pp. 286–295.

the criteria of performance

The private economy, as noted above, utilizes a clear test of performance: profits. Moreover, competition enforces the application of this test and casts out the failures. While the profit criterion is highly satisfactory for most economic activity, it has shortcomings where there are significant externalities, decreasing costs, and imperfect competition.

In the public economy, the application of criteria falls short on two counts. First, there is the lack of necessity to apply any test of performance. Responsible governments will, of course, make a greater effort in this respect than irresponsible governments, but applying the test is neither automatic nor inevitable. The alertness and motivations of politicians, administrators, and the public determine with what zeal and consistency standards of performance are applied.

Second, there is the confusion over what criteria to use. The public economy suffers, not from a shortage of criteria, but from an overabundance. Many separate standards can be proposed: standards of quality of output produced or of service rendered, of quantity of output or service; standards of the correctness of the proportions in which they are produced, of the diversity or choice offered, of innovations or experiments to be tried; standards for minimizing costs. But a way of applying all these standards simultaneously has not been found. The profit test, which approximates a summation of all these standards, is the nearest thing to a solution we have. The public economy, where it applies standards, does so one at a time, specifying, for example, the cost but not the quantity of output, or the quantity of output but not the cost.[3] For the appropriate amount of diversity, or for specifications of quality, the public economy is adrift without a compass.

In the face of these difficulties, the tendency to fall back on

[3] An attempt to combine the two, the *performance budget,* which specifies both the cost and the quantity of service to be performed, is a crude mechanism, unsuccessful because of the difficulties of both detailing the service expected and knowing whether the cost permitted was actually the minimum attainable.

the profit calculation is strong. Public economy can no doubt frequently be improved by simulating the profit standard of private enterprise. But unless managers are permitted to be independent and to pursue the objective of profit maximization and unless profit is adhered to as the decisive test of performance, the profit calculation degenerates into a meaningless exercise.

government antipathy to competition and diversity

Though the government can perform a vital function in sustaining competition among private firms, it is inherently antipathetic to competition or diversity in the affairs it administers itself. Cases of government ownership in which the government divorces itself from administration by entrusting operations to wholly independent managers are obviously not at issue here. What is at issue is that the government is rarely willing to grant independence to its managers. To most of its advocates, the essence of government intervention is that policy shall be determined by the government, and not by government agents behaving like private entrepreneurs. To the extent that decision-making power is delegated to separate units, a degree of competition, diversity, and experimentation is possible. But it is in the nature of bureaucratic hierarchy that subordinates must conform to a set of rules and must be subject to the supervision of the top level of the hierarchy. It is difficult, for example, to imagine local postmasters being permitted to experiment with new equipment.

The private economy, though also subject to the bureaucratic problem within large organizations, greatly reduces the problem by having many independent organizations.[4] Furthermore, the subordinate units of a private organization can be permitted considerable independence because it can use the profit test, which imposes an ultimate judgment and control on

[4] Similarly, independent governments like state or local governments permit greater diversity in the programs they administer (like education) than is possible in a program of the central government. How much society benefits from the diversity depends on whether the customers intelligently evaluate the choices available and can exercise their choice.

each unit. The government agency, lacking a clear basis for evaluating performance, cannot be so free in delegating power to its subordinate units.

A second reason for government antipathy to competition is the political process. Given the opportunity to insulate themselves from competition, not many will resist it. Government intervention in the economy creates that opportunity. Political pressure then builds up to limit competition. The anti-competition pattern that develops will depend on the relative political strengths of the pressure groups and on popular attitudes. Where power is more or less evenly distributed and antagonism to monopoly is not an established public attitude, government encouragement of cartelization throughout the country may result. In the United States, where hostility to monopoly is strong, but concentrated almost entirely on "big business," we find the contradictory policies of government antitrust action in the field of large-scale business and government action to restrict competition in small business and the professions. Licensing in the professions (doctors, pharmacists, accountants, barbers, and many others),[5] licensing of taxis, resale-price-maintenance laws, building codes, and restrictions on the movement of milk between states or localities are among the devices by which the government, under the guise of public protection, restrains competition. The end result is inescapable: The urge to evade the obligation to compete will, wherever government intervention in the economy creates the opportunity, thrust into the political compromise an element of restriction of competition.

One of the most striking examples of the destructive effect

[5] "One may not be surprised to learn that pharmacists, accountants, and dentists have been reached by state law as have sanitarians and psychologists, assayers and architects, veterinarians and librarians. But with what joy of discovery does one learn about the licensing of threshing machine operators and dealers in scrap tobacco? What of egg graders and guide dog trainers, pest controllers and yacht salesmen, tree surgeons and well diggers, tile layers and potato growers?" Walter Gellhorn, *Individual Freedom and Governmental Restraints* (Baton Rouge, La.: Louisiana State University Press, 1956), p. 106; quoted in Milton Friedman, *Capitalism and Freedom* (Chicago: The University of Chicago Press, 1962), p. 139.

on competition of government intervention is the behavior of the Interstate Commerce Commission. Originally created to regulate railroads because of the insufficiency of competition, the agency now zealously devotes itself to limiting competition among and within the railroad, trucking, air, and shipping industries.[6] This perversion of purpose has become so ludicrous that railroads now place newspaper advertisements appealing for the right to reduce their rates.[7] Evidently the regulators of industry, like its managers, find their work easier and their life pleasanter without competition.

uncertainty and risk taking

One of the advantages claimed for centralized decision making is that it reduces secondary uncertainty—the uncertainty of one unit in a decentralized system about the intentions of other units. (No valid claim can be made that centralization reduces primary uncertainty.) [8]

While it is true that *complete* centralization would eliminate secondary uncertainty, government decision making in fact does not eliminate it, since economic control is never completely centralized. The magnitude and complexity of economic administration require that, even in a government-directed economy, a large part of the decision making must be delegated to subordinate government agencies and to the managements of enterprises.

Thus, secondary uncertainty persists in a government-directed economy. Moreover, it may be a greater source of economic inefficiency than in a market economy. In a market system the objectives of firms and the principles on which they base their decisions are known, and consequently their behavior has a fair degree of predictability. The objectives and operating rules of government agencies are considerably more

---

[6] See Walter Adams, "The Role of Competition in the Regulated Industries," *American Economic Review*, vol. 48, no. 2 (May, 1958), pp. 527–543; Lucille Sheppard Keyes, "The Protective Functions of Commission Regulation," *ibid.*, pp. 544–552.

[7] *The New York Times*, June 10, 1963.

[8] See p. 51.

uncertain, and their behavior is correspondingly more difficult to predict. Consequently, a decision-making unit in a government-directed economy may be more uncertain about the behavior of other units than it would be if it were operating in a market system. One reflection of this uncertainty is the high level of inventories which managers in non-market economies attempt to hold because of the unpredictability of the flow in their supplies.

In the treatment of risk, every government is in a dilemma. If government decision makers do not share in the risks, they are likely to make insufficient allowance for risk in their calculations. Thus, the public authority who thinks he will not have to pay for his errors can gamble on grandiose projects with inadequate research and against long odds.[9] If, on the other hand, public officials were to pay for their errors by loss of position or status, excessive caution would be the probable result. Public service cannot offer the kind of inducement for risk taking which, in private enterprise, is provided by potential profits.

irrationality

The failure of individuals to maximize their welfare because of their incapacity to make optimal choices [10] has its counterpart in governmental decisions. If the public choices are arrived at by democratic process, the irrationalities that afflicted private decisions now find expression by influencing group decisions. If the public choices are arrived at by non-democratic process and represent choices imposed by leaders, they then embody the irrationalities of those leaders. We have no evidence that authoritarian positions are filled by any method that assures more rationality than would be obtained by a random selection from the population. Indeed, history, including the most recent, provides abundant evidence for the contrary argument.

[9] For example, Khrushchev's "virgin lands" scheme, a program launched in 1959 for growing corn in the Soviet Union on a vast area of land previously thought to be unsuited to cultivation. The previous thoughts proved to be correct.
[10] See pp. 19–20.

While an element of irrationality can be found in people whether they are making private or public choices, there is a crucial distinction between private and public in the much greater scope for exercising irrationality that public action affords. Society evades unpleasant economic adjustments if it can, much as people put off a visit to the dentist; and it yields, if permitted, to some temptations against its better judgment. However, private choice, being made in the market, is subject to the impersonal and objective rules of the market, which prohibit the most damaging types of irrationality. Public choice, on the other hand, is free of the market rules, and that freedom permits anomalies like agricultural price-support programs, steel plants built for prestige, ideological rejection of the interest rate as a tool of economic calculations, adoption of organizational forms and industry structures on doctrinal rather than economic grounds (collectives, cooperatives, cottage industry, small-scale units, large-scale units), restrictions on competition among products or occupations under the illusion that it is possible for everyone to climb up on the backs of others, and innumerable other failures of society to act in its own best interest. It is possible, of course, to argue that none of these is actually a case of irrationality—with only a little ingenuity one can propose a rationale for each—but, then, one can do the same for all the cases of alleged private irrationality.

corruption

Government intervention necessarily endows its administrators with power. The authority to regulate, to grant licenses and permits, to place orders, to fill positions puts the administrators in the position of giving away a valuable right or asset which, in the private economy, is either free to all or exchanged in an open competitive market. It should occasion no surprise that instead of giving away "his" asset the administrator sells it and pockets the proceeds. Whether power corrupts or whether it merely opens the door to existing corruption, the fact is that power and corruption appear together.

Cases of the same sort can be found in the private economy. For example, purchasing agents have favors which they are in a position to sell. But competition in private business limits the extent of such private power, and the motives of business provide a constant inducement to expose and check these practices.[11] The distinction between the private and public economy on this score is significant. Corruption, with all its economic and moral costs, rises as increased government intervention expands the opportunities for it.

SECONDARY WARTS

In the private economy, certain defects are seen to exist even with perfect organization and administration of the market. The problem of externalities is an example. Other defects— those of an organizational or administrative type like imperfect competition or imperfect information—can be assumed away for theoretical purposes, but as a practical matter they must be regarded as permanent characteristics of the market. Similarly, in the public economy, the six defects discussed in the previous pages must be regarded as inherent. In addition, there are the defects which can be assumed away by postulating perfect organization and administration but which, in practice, cannot be eradicated. Physicists make an equivalent distinction: "Some things never happen in the physical world because they are *impossible;* others because they are too *improbable.* The laws which forbid the first are primary laws; the laws which forbid the second are secondary laws." [12] The administrative

[11] "There is no evidence that conflicts of interest are more successfully resolved in the business world than they are in political life, but I conjecture they are better handled in industry. There are rewards for the superior or subordinate who detects malfeasance in business, whereas the rewards for the detection of double dealing in political life go chiefly to the people out of power—precisely those who are least well situated to detect it." George J. Stigler, "The Economics of Conflict of Interest," *Journal of Political Economy,* vol. 75, no. 1 (February, 1967), p. 101.

[12] A. S. Eddington, *The Nature of the Physical World* (London: Cambridge University Press, 1928), p. 75; quoted in Karl R. Popper, *The Logic of Scientific Discovery* (New York: Basic Books, Inc., Publishers, 1959), p. 203.

impediments to optimization in the public economy may be called "secondary" defects, not in the sense that they are less important or less injurious, but in the sense that it is possible though too improbable that a government-directed economy might be free of them.

Administrative problems—difficulties of gathering information, reaching decisions, communicating, supervising, evaluating, correcting—are found in any type of economy. However, the market, through its system of price signals and profit criterion, performs or greatly simplifies the work of economic administration. The administrative burden increases as government control supplants the market, reaching its peak in the economy which is intended to be wholly controlled by the central government or "centrally planned."

The nature of the administrative problem in the public economy can be seen most clearly by beginning with the case of centralized planning. The application to intermediate cases of government intervention will then be fairly obvious.

the impossibility of complete centralization

The administration of an economy requires a vast number of adjustments continuously. Input and output decisions must respond to changes in consumer preferences, government preferences, technology, foreign demand, weather, accidents, mechanical breakdowns, and miscalculations. An immense amount of information possessed by consumers, managers, and technicians should enter into the total decision-making process. In a market system individual decision makers are permitted to respond spontaneously to the data that concern them, using the information which they have on hand or which they gather. This large number of information gatherers and decision makers, interacting with each other at many levels, can make great numbers of adjustments in a short period of time.

In a centrally directed economy, individuals are not permitted to adjust to each other. The data must be piped upward to the central authority. Decisions must be reached and orders regulating adjustments must be passed down again. The number of adjustments that can be accomplished in a short time by this form of organization is comparatively limited. Faced with the great number of adjustments that must be made, a system of completely centralized control, with its restricted capacity for making adjustments, must be expected to break down. "[A] centrally directed industrial system is administratively impossible—impossible in the same sense in which it is impossible for a cat to swim the Atlantic." [13]

central control and the price system

One approach to dealing with the immense administrative task of operating a centrally controlled economy is to use the price mechanism to carry part of the burden. Proposals have been made for a simulated market system which, while basically centralized, would permit part of the management of the economy to be decentralized.[14] In the simulated market system, prices of inputs and outputs would be set by the central agency. Managers would be instructed to take these prices as given and to produce, by the least-cost method, the output which would maximize profits. In effect, the managers would be instructed to behave like entrepreneurs in a purely competitive market. The central agency, observing the aggregate effects of producers' and consumers' decisions, would have the task of adjusting the price structure so as to equate supply and demand for each output and each input. In this system, either consumers' preferences could be allowed to rule or the central agency, by further price adjustments, could impose authorities' preferences. In addition, the central agency could adjust prices so that they reflect social rather than private costs and benefits (in cases where social and private measures diverge).

The simulated market system would relieve the central agency of the need to collect the information which managers have about factory conditions, technological possibilities, con-

---

[13] Michael Polanyi, *The Logic of Liberty* (London: Routledge & Kegan Paul, Ltd., 1951), p. 126. See pp. 111–137 for a more complete and formalized discussion of the administrative impossibility of completely centralized direction of an economy.

[14] See, for example, Oskar Lange, *On the Economic Theory of Socialism* (Minneapolis: The University of Minnesota Press, 1938).

sumer preferences, and other matters. It would permit many input and output decisions to be made by the managers, these price decisions being coordinated and rationalized by the price calculations. Nevertheless, the administrative burden on the central agency would still be immense. The central agency would have to keep watch over the markets for a great number of outputs and inputs, issuing a constant stream of orders for price adjustments. (The system is probably workable, however, if continuous price review is not attempted and a degree of price rigidity is accepted. The degree of inefficiency that results depends, of course, on how distorted prices are permitted to become. Special arrangements to decentralize pricing might be made in the case of perishable items or other products where the waste of price rigidity would be acute.)

The simulated market system in its pure form has not been adopted anywhere. It has little appeal to the planning theorist, who seeks to replace the decentralized trial-and-error method of the market with the comprehensive analysis and final optimal solution of the Plan. The practical politician and his economic advisers, once they are ready to accept decentralization, seem to find it preferable to go beyond the simulated market system and adopt something close to a genuine market system.[15] Yugoslavia, for example, has moved toward a system in

[15] Readiness to accept decentralization naturally comes only slowly to those accustomed to wielding great economic power. Their underlying attitude is summed up by an insightful comment on the Burmese economy: "It was precisely this miracle of the market mechanism, which can inspire awe among Western students, that disturbed Burmese the most. For they saw in the theory the possibility of impersonal forces, an 'invisible hand,' making decisions which would control their own actions. By accepting the logic of profits, apparently powerful people would have to give in to the demands of the common public; thus instead of controlling the public and dominating events, they would have to serve the public and respond to events. The Burmese preference is for a less impersonal and deterministic method of allocating resources, and hence they have generally favored political forms of decision making for guiding investments." Lucian W. Pye, *Politics, Personality, and Nation Building: Burma's Search for Identity* (New Haven, Conn.: Yale University Press, 1962), p. 170.

The predictable reaction of a powerful official to the market mechanism is illustrated by Lionel Robbins's story of the highly placed man

which enterprise managers have considerable independence in making pricing, production, and investment decisions, with profits as the chief guideline.

the middle morass

Most of the state-operated economies, having found complete centralization unworkable but being unwilling to swing over to a market system, have been stumbling about in the treacherous area in between. The Soviet Union began at one extreme—a disastrous attempt (1919-1921) to approximate central direction [16]—and since then has been moving back and forth: to a decentralized market system (the NEP), back toward centralization, and now apparently toward decentralization. Poland, Hungary, and Czechoslovakia have drifted from a point near the central-control extreme toward forms of decentralization.

In all these cases the pretense has had to be abandoned that the Plan is a statement of the inputs and outputs of the various sectors for the coming period, based on exact calculations to assure the internal consistency and optimal quality of the allocations. Of necessity, decision-making authority has been granted to plant managers. The output figures of the Plan become, not the definite requirements for a calculated ideal solution, but targets, and encouragement and rewards go to the managers who violate the Plan by exceeding their output targets. The quality and composition of the output, to a considerable degree, have had to be left to the plant managers. Even investment decisions have, to some extent, been delegated to

---

in a collectivist state to whom he explained the idea of the simulated market: "The great man looked very unhappy. 'I have no use for that,' he grumbled. 'That's not my idea of how to run industry. I want industries organized as a whole so that'—and here he waved expressive hands—'I can say to this industry, "You expand," and to that industry, "You contract."'" *The Economic Problem in Peace and War* (London: Macmillan & Co., Ltd., 1947), p. 79.

It is strong testimony of the inefficiency of central control relative to the market system that, despite the well-entrenched opposition, the economies of the Communist countries of Eastern Europe are being pushed toward the market method.

[16] Polanyi, *op. cit.*, pp. 126–133.

the plant level. Moreover, to make the system work, local management in overcentralized systems has had to wink at the rules, substitute its own judgment for that of the central agency, and engage in illegal transactions with other units to bypass the central hierarchy.[17]

The so-called centrally planned economies are, then, actually mixed systems of centralized control and mutual adjustment by decentralized decision makers. The decentralized decisions require, for calculation and coordination, a set of price signals. For proper motivation of managers and for evaluation of their performances, a profit calculation is needed. Unfortunately, without free markets to determine prices, the prices actually used for calculations bear no close or consistent relation to the information which prices are intended to signal. With arbitrary prices and interference from above in management decisions, the profit calculation becomes a meaningless test.

Therein lies the source of the muddle that afflicts this type of economy—the necessity for market techniques but the unwillingness to be governed by the markets.[18]

the information gap

The correctness of any decision, private or governmental, depends on the quality of the information available to the decision maker. In the most exalted vision of government economic management—where, as Wiles puts it, perfect competition is replaced by perfect computation [19]—the quantity of information required vastly exceeds what is needed for private decision making, for the government decision is supposedly based not only on the consequences for those directly involved

---

[17] ". . . within the *unintended* gaps of the Soviet system of planned economy, a rudimentary system of spontaneous co-ordination has emerged. It is a hidden, secret, fragmentary, cramped and contorted sort of market economy—but it exists and must exist as long as the aspiration to totalitarian planning exists." Edward Shils, in Congress for Cultural Freedom, *The Soviet Economy* (London: Martin Secker & Warburg, Ltd., 1956), pp. 97–98.

[18] Examples of the misallocations that result are given in the next chapter

[19] P. J. D. Wiles, *The Political Economy of Communism* (Oxford: Basil Blackwell, 1962), p. 147.

(which is the basis of the decentralized decision) but also on all the other costs and benefits, which are external to those who would be the parties in decentralized decisions. Even in less ambitious government efforts, the case for government intervention frequently rests on the greater information that centralized decisions will utilize, relative to decentralized decisions.

But, while the demand for information in centralized decisions is greater, the supply is less. The bulk of the information needed for economic decisions is initially in the possession of the individuals or units at the bottom of the organizational pyramid: Consumers and workers know their preferences; managers and technicians know about their production possibilities; research organizations, scientists, local government bodies, and others have relevant information. In a system of centralized decisions, all this information is supposedly collected and analyzed at the top. However, the collection process, which is unnecessary in decentralized systems, involves a cost which puts a severe constraint on the quantity of information that the central agency can obtain. The cost is especially heavy in the form of delay in reaching decisions while information is being collected. Moreover, much of the information is "perishable," becoming stale in a relatively short time and going to waste if not acted on quickly. Some information at the lower levels will never be centrally collected because the cost of collection in resources and time is prohibitive. Thus a large part of the information which is used in decentralized decisions is wasted in a centralized system either because it is never collected at all or because it spoils before it can be used.

It is true that data gathering is being improved and accelerated by technological advances. But the amount of information to be gathered also increases as the economy becomes more complex and the number of choices multiplies. We cannot predict the eventual outcome of this race, but we can safely say that information collecting is not going to become costless and that the information available to a central agency will always have to be rationed.

In addition to the information which is obtainable but costly to collect, the designs for centralized decisions ordinarily call for information which cannot be obtained at all. Knowledge about the future which will dispel primary uncertainty plays a large part in descriptions of central planning, but this information is no more available to a central agency than to individual units.

A second type of information which is unobtainable in precise form is the valuation of those benefits and costs on which the market does not put a value. One of the supposedly key contributions of planning—the correction for externalities—arises because external benefits and costs are not registered in the market, and central decision makers therefore attempt to estimate them so that they can be taken into account. Unfortunately non-market valuations involve a degree of guesswork and judgment which puts a severe strain on the objectivity of those who make these valuations and on those who use them for decisions.

The pliability of non-market valuations removes one of the restraints on uneconomic decisions. Does the Minister of Electrification want an atomic power plant to add to his glory? Calculate the costs, using a low enough interest rate, and perhaps it will appear economic. If not, throw in something for the value of the research that may be generated by the atomic venture and for the value of the stimulating effect of this symbol of progress.

the failure in international exchange

The inability of a centrally directed economy to arrive at a structure of prices that will correctly measure the relative values and costs of products, and the insistence of the planners on predetermining events rather than developing the ability of the economy to adjust to events, have their most damaging effects in the sphere of international exchange.

Unless the price structure can be relied on to measure more or less accurately the relative values and costs of products, it becomes impossible for planners to calculate whether international exchange will yield a gain or a loss for their country. There is an excellent chance that a country engaging in international exchange on the basis of a distorted price structure will make some exchanges that actually lower its national income. Only in the case of products at the extremes of the comparative-advantage spectrum can the planners feel any confidence in the correctness of their decisions. In the intermediate zone, where the authorities are uncertain whether they will gain or lose from trade, the pursuit of international exchange will hold little attraction.

An even stronger bias against international trade is instilled by the incompatibility of international trade with the type of planning favored by centrally directed economies. International trade introduces the variables of foreign demand and supply, which are outside the control of the national planners; it increases the difficulty of prearranging production schedules and puts a premium on the adjustability of the economy to external events. Central planning, preferring the greater certainty of a closed economy and lacking the adjustability of a market economy, leans inevitably toward trade restrictions.[20]

the forecasting fallacies

Firmly entrenched in planning literature are the twin ideas that central planning is distinguished from the market system by its use of forecasting and that central planning has a special advantage in forecasting.[21] The previous chapter pointed out that economic decision making, whether decentralized or cen-

[20] The damaging effects of this and other defects in central planning are neatly illustrated by comparing the vastly inferior performance of the East German to the West German economy, though they started with very similar cultures and factor endowments. See Wolfgang F. Stolper, "Planning and International Integration in Soviet Germany," *Banca Nazionale del Lavoro Quarterly Review,* vol. 14, no. 57 (June, 1961), pp. 184–196.

[21] For example, in this criticism of the simulated market system: "This system in fact allows the mechanism of adjustments after the event characteristic of competitive economy and of capitalism to survive. The task of *foreseeing* (and foresight is necessary in every economic system which is not purely static) is not entrusted to a central organ capable, by its very position, of taking an overall view of the various consequences, short-term and long-term, that its decisions may have. . . ." Charles Bettelheim, *Studies in the Theory of Planning* (New York: Asia Publishing House, 1959), p. 32.

tralized, contains an element of forecasting, and that the supposed advantage of centralized decision making is not its superiority in forecasting but its curtailment of the need for forecasting. Central planning is intended to eliminate secondary uncertainty—uncertainty of each producing unit about the intentions of the other producing units—and thereby eliminate the need of each unit to forecast the behavior of the others.[22]

The second forecasting fallacy which appears in much of the literature on planning is that a centrally planned economy enjoys a superiority in forecasting which enables it to reduce *primary* uncertainty—uncertainty arising from any cause other than the decentralization of producers' decisions. It should be obvious that there is nothing about central direction which reduces the difficulty of forecasting changes in the society's preferences, changes in technical knowledge, or economic disturbances coming from abroad. This fallacy originates in a confusion between reducing primary uncertainty and ignoring it. When the Planning Commission establishes the bill of goods to be available to consumers in the next period, it is no more engaged in forecasting than a prison warden who states what his prisoners will have for breakfast tomorrow morning. He is not forecasting consumer preference. He is ignoring it. When the Planning Commission schedules the technology that will be used in the future, it is not forecasting unknown technical possibilities. It is ignoring them.

The problem of decision making under uncertainty cannot be met by seeking certainty or by pretending to have found it.[23] The methods of dealing with uncertainty are varied, but

[22] Since centralization cannot be complete, secondary uncertainty is not eliminated by planning; it may, in fact, be increased. See pp. 64–65.

[23] "The principles of logic and mathematics represent the only domain in which certainty is attainable; but these principles are analytic and empty. *Certainty is inseparable from emptiness.*" Quoted from Hans Reichenbach, *The Rise of Scientific Philosophy* (Berkeley, Calif.: University of California Press, 1957), pp. 303–304, by G. H. Fisher, "Aspects of Corporate Planning in Defense Industry," in J. A. Stockfish (ed.), *Planning and Forecasting in the Defense Industries* (Belmont, Calif.: Wadsworth Publishing Co., 1962), p. 82. Fisher adds: "So it is in the realm of long-range corporate planning. If we approach problems in a spirit of the 'quest for certainty,' we are likely to end up with 'empty' results."

chief among them are techniques for maintaining flexibility and adjustability of decisions, as circumstances unfold. In this respect central planning, with its rigid schedules and overburdened administrative apparatus, is at a distinct disadvantage compared with the market system.

5 | planning in developed countries

The reasons why it is impossible for the state to make optimal economic decisions were discussed in the previous chapter. These points can now be illustrated by examining a number of cases of government intervention which are generally labeled, rightly or wrongly, "planning." This chapter is restricted to the advanced economies—those where the institutions, skills, and attitudes required by a dynamic exchange economy are not drastically lacking. The special problems of backward economies are treated in the next chapter.

LAND-USE PLANNING

One of the few instances of government planning, in the strict sense previously defined, that can be found in the advanced free-enterprise countries is land-use planning. The use of land presents a particularly acute problem of external costs or benefits. When individuals are located close together, the use which any one party makes of land affects the welfare of his neighbors, and the costs or benefits to the neighbors are external to the calculation of the decision-making party.

One approach to this problem is to regulate the more notorious causes of external costs like pollution of air or water. But dealing with any substantial part of the externalities associated with land use requires urban or regional planning on a comprehensive scale.

In its earliest and most elementary stage, urban planning was concerned with preventing incompatible uses (a slaughterhouse in a residential area) and regulating the height and density of construction. The instrument for implementing this kind of planning is the zoning laws. This limited concept, however, fell short of the planning ideal on a variety of counts. One important omission was the provision for open space. Though it has been suggested that zoning should have allocated land to open space,[1] in actuality zoning is not an appropriate method. Equity and freedom from arbitrary decisions require that all landholders within a given zone be treated alike, a principle which would be violated by forbidding construction on designated areas within a zone. Some areas may be zoned for agriculture only, but even then, unless the land is to be frozen into an uneconomic and underutilized pattern, exceptions will probably have to be granted eventually. The only satisfactory method of providing for open use is public purchase of land for that purpose.

Another important planning objective omitted in a purely zoning approach to planning is the protection of aesthetic, historical, and cultural values of urban areas. The individual's decision to build or to tear down does not necessarily take into account the cost to others of unaesthetic construction or the destruction of buildings of historical, cultural, or aesthetic value, although instances of a sense of responsibility to the public can certainly be found. Aesthetic regulation and the protection of existing buildings that form part of society's precious heritage are primarily a public responsibility and one fraught with the greatest difficulties.

A third urban problem that has traditionally been presumed to create a need for planning is the blighted area. A spot of decay, in the form of deteriorated housing or unattractive atmosphere, tends to spread as the established residents leave and are replaced by lower-income groups, and property owners discontinue the maintenance of buildings. No individual

[1] Carl Feiss, "Planning Absorbs Zoning," *Journal of the American Institute of Planners*, vol. 27, no. 2 (May, 1961), pp. 121–126.

property owner can stop the spread of blight or rehabilitate the area once the blight has taken hold. Collective action affords the only solution. So, at least, runs the usual analysis. Actually, run-down areas have been rehabilitated without collective action (the Georgetown area in Washington, D.C.), and other areas with spots of decay manage to resist the spread of blight. In general, the root of the problem of blight is not in decentralized decision making but in the cultural and income characteristics of the section of the population which makes slums of the areas in which they live. Until education and economic advancement have eradicated the slum makers, a blighted area can be rehabilitated only by shifting the population to blight another area. Once education and economic advancement have done their work, private decentralized motivations will be adequate to correct blight.[2] This is not to deny that the government can make a contribution to the elimination of slums but only to say that it cannot do so by tearing down buildings and putting up new buildings.[3]

From its early aim of improving cities, urban planning branched out toward the objective of destroying them. The problems of cities were to be met by scattering them, dividing the population into a number of smaller, self-contained communities separated from each other by open areas. This goal of disintegrating the great city into "garden cities" represented, not the despair of planners at the task of bringing the city

[2] See Jane Jacobs, *The Death and Life of Great American Cities* (New York: Random House, Inc., 1961), chap. 15, on areas that "unslum" themselves. "The processes that occur in unslumming depend on the fact that a metropolitan economy, if it is working well, is constantly transforming many poor people into middle-class people, many illiterates into skilled (or even educated) people, many greenhorns into competent citizens [p. 288]."

[3] The notion (which underlies slum-clearance programs) that the aging of buildings makes slums, is undoubtedly incorrect. Areas with old buildings and low rents need not be slums. See, for example, the description of the West End in Boston, in Herbert J. Gans, "The Human Implications of Current Redevelopment and Relocation Planning," *Journal of the American Institute of Planners*, vol. 25, no. 1 (February, 1959), pp. 15–25. The causation is the reverse: The buildings are allowed to deteriorate or are not modernized because the area is becoming a slum.

closer to the desires of its residents, but their preference for imposing their own ideas of the good life. The antagonism that many intellectuals had long felt for cities,[4] and their romantic belief in the capacity of the countryside to cure society's ills, found expression in the garden-city movement.

It was not many years, however, before the attention of city planners was turned from decentralizing the city to the question of how to recentralize it. Decentralization had been greatly accelerated by an unforeseen turn of events—the transportation revolution caused by the automobile. The automobile seemed to offer the opportunity to combine living in the country with easy access to the city for work or recreation, and the exodus to the suburbs was rapid. The planner's repugnance to the city was now replaced by his repugnance to the non-city, the urban sprawl that ate up the countryside, spawned endless traffic problems, and sapped the life of the core of the city—which was discovered, by comparison with the suburbs, to be well worth preserving after all. Planning to renew the central city and conserve the open land around the city then became the order of the day.

How has land-use planning worked out in practice? I am not asking how wisely governments have made decisions involving the use of land in carrying out the normal government functions like roadbuilding, the creation of parks, or the location of public buildings. These collective decisions, like private decisions, require study, the weighing of alternatives, the application of whatever foresight is possible; but these elements of the decision process are not what should be meant by "planning." What I am asking is: How successful have the efforts been to overcome the defects in land use that result from the decentralization of decisions, and the efforts to produce superior results by centralized controls which take full account of the external impact of each land-use decision?

The answer must be that the results have fallen far short of the planning vision. In part the shortcomings can be attributed to errors arising from inexperience, which can be corrected as planners learn from their errors. The major blame, however,

[4] See Morton and Lucia White, *The Intellectual versus the City* (Cambridge, Mass.: Harvard University Press and the M.I.T. Press, 1962).

falls on those stumbling blocks inherent in government decision making that are outlined in the previous chapter. A blend of the conflict of objectives, imperfect foresight, and the imprecise valuation of external costs, explains most of the failure.

In the case of planning through zoning, the aims are modest and the extent of the disappointment correspondingly moderate. Zoning prevents most of the worst abuses of mixed land use and, on the whole, probably does more good than harm. Nevertheless, it is far from ideal, for it is a clumsy instrument to handle a complicated problem. Zoning must dictate a pattern of land use for an uncertain future. To permit some flexibility in the face of this uncertainty, it must include some procedure for considering exceptions to or changes in the zoning plan. But the granting of variances opens the way to the erosion of the zoning plan through political trading, corruption, or simple ignorance on the part of the zoning board. Finding a wholly satisfactory middle path between a rigid plan consistently maintained and a flexible plan peppered with violations is more than can be expected. A further problem which has been beyond the power of zoning plans to solve is the balance between diversity and uniformity. Some degree of diversity in land use is highly desirable for both convenience and attractiveness, but zoning is essentially an instrument for imposing conformity. Long experience with zoning has revealed its inherent defects:

> Its first defect is that it is a gross device for handling delicate problems. In preventing gross abuses, it simultaneously obstructs major innovations. In pursuit of consistency it often becomes arbitrary and is tolerated only by the presence of a counterpoised board of appeals which facilitates violation. It stands in monumental intolerance of mixed land uses, and in attempting to control nuisance it equally prevents the surprise and delight of well-mannered variety. However accidentally, it promotes unmitigated uniformity and substitutes minimum standards for human conscience; and bare adequacy supplants human aspiration. Often enough it protects property values at the cost

> of more generous human values. . . . In an age of ac-
> celerated change it attempts to induce premature equilib-
> rium, but it cannot so stand, for the patching of zoning
> ordinances continues to pace the *ad hoc* patching of the
> communities themselves.[5]

The protection of the aesthetic and historical qualities of
cities has been a more conspicuous failure of governments.
Collective taste is not superior to private taste; and the taste of
government officials, to judge from public buildings, is, if anything, worse. Hence, aside from the practical difficulties of
agreeing on aesthetic standards and enforcing them without
tyranny, one can feel little confidence that public intervention
in the aesthetics of construction will bring about an improvement. Certain rather obvious measures could probably be
agreed upon and administered without undue arbitrariness,
like regulations on outdoor advertising. On the whole, however, the public impact on aesthetics is not promising. This is
particularly so when aesthetics comes into conflict with other
objectives of government. The prime case of this sort is the
government's concern for the flow of traffic: The appearance
of the city has rarely been allowed to stand in the way of elevated highways, interchanges, road widening, or the other
monstrosities of road transportation.

Similar comments apply to the preservation of property of
historical value. In the contest between tradition and change,
governments have generally behaved, at best, like reluctant
defenders of the historical heritage. Where by good fortune
buildings have survived until their great value has become
clear (frequently by the yardstick of their commercial value as
a tourist attraction), governments commonly protect them. But
those survivors of the past which are still in the intermediate
ripening stage, when foresight and a sense of history are needed
to recognize their irreplaceable value to the future, have not
noticeably benefited from government protection. In such
cases, the defense of the past usually devolves upon individuals

[5] James E. Lee, "The Role of the Planner in the Present," *Journal of the
American Institute of Planners*, vol. 24, no. 3 (1958), p. 153.

and private institutions, while the government, with its greater powers for large-scale land clearance, is the chief vandal.[6]

The matter of aesthetic and historical values is essentially one of a conflict of interest among private groups or between private groups and the government, which has its own land-use objectives. In this conflict, there is no strong reason to expect the government to calculate the external aesthetic and historical costs and to compensate the losers. Indeed, a common government complaint is that, if it must fully compensate the losers, it will not be able to carry out its program.[7] Nor is there any good reason to expect that when the government regulates a private decision, it will permit aesthetic-historical considerations to frustrate other government objectives.[8] The beauty of cities demands restraints on government by individuals as much as restraints on individuals by government.

Land-use planning has been put to its major test by the disintegrating force of the automobile. By and large it has failed the test. The problem is essentially this: The limited transportation facilities which once made great numbers of people prefer to concentrate in cities have now been replaced by the extremely flexible and convenient transportation system of the automobile. The possibility of living outside the city but retaining ready access to the economic and cultural life of the city, a combination which has proved to be powerfully attractive, is vastly enhanced by the spread of automobile ownership and the highway network. The result has been an outward migration from the cities to the suburbs, especially among the

[6] For an illustrative case of major public vandalism, note the scheduled destruction of historic Lafayette Square in Washington, to put up some government office buildings. *The New York Times,* Feb. 14, 1962, p. 37. (Subsequently President Kennedy intervened to preserve substantially the attractive features of the area.)

[7] For example, the Town and Country Planning Act of 1947 (Britain) is said to have been designed to "meet the ever-present fear of need to pay compensation which constitutes an ever-present threat to bold planning." Charles M. Harr, *Land Planning in a Free Society* (Cambridge, Mass.: Harvard University Press, 1951), p. 101.

[8] One instance of an influential government objective is the shift of tax-exempt property to the tax rolls. Some California towns have even sold existing park areas. " 'Slurbs' Assailed by Californians," *The New York Times,* Jan. 14, 1962.

middle-income and upper-income groups. The process has now gone sufficiently far that three characteristics of the eventual outcome, not generally foreseen at the outset, have become clear. (1) The qualities which are attracting migrants to the suburbs will largely disappear as the migration proceeds. Open land vanishes as suburban single-family housing (which is extremely land-consuming) expands. As land scarcity increases and cost rises, apartment construction begins to replace the single unit. The suburbs then spread ever outward in search of cheap open land. Taxes rise as suburban population becomes more concentrated and demands more public services. The dream of inexpensive housing in a semi-rural setting, with the central city only a brief ride away, becomes steadily more remote. (2) The central city decays as shopping moves to the suburbs. Blighted areas appear when the departing population is replaced by immigrants with depressed incomes, untrained in the urban way of life, and with the unconcern of the rootless for the appearance and reputation of their neighborhoods. The deterioration of the city accelerates the outward movement of the higher-income group. (3) Transportation problems multiply but get no nearer to solution. As the road systems expand, the use of public transportation falls, which raises the cost per passenger and leads to a decline in the quality of services and a rise in price. Traffic increases as more passengers shift to automobiles. More road building to meet the traffic increase repeats the process. In addition, the more the road system is improved, the greater the outspread of population and the more the roads are used. Road construction eats up land in both the cities and the suburbs, and intensifies the outward movement of the urban boundaries. Traffic always expands to overload whatever new road capacity is constructed.

One can foresee the ultimate equilibrium position of these forces, the dispersion of the central city, and the filling up of the surrounding area, until the two are hardly distinguishable and equally undistinguished. Neither those who love cities nor those who enjoy the open countryside will have what they want, and it is hard to imagine who will want what he will have.

The natural answer to a problem of this sort seems to be

planning, and, indeed, it has given rise to urban and regional planning efforts in the United States on a grand scale. The results have not been encouraging.

With regard to the conservation of open space, the first and most obvious step would be for the local government to acquire land for open use, maintaining it as park land or leasing it for agriculture. Almost nothing has been done in this direction. For one thing, it would be an unpopular move with those who intend to move to the suburbs and who would object to measures that would increase the scarcity and cost of land. Second, the public is generally unwilling to bear the cost of acquiring and maintaining the land. If the basic planning premise is correct—that the benefits of public acquisition of open land will substantially exceed the costs—then the public attitude is irrational. Unfortunately, there is no reason why collective choice should be any more rational than private choice.

The second urban-planning objective—to rehabilitate the central city—would serve the dual purpose of slowing the rate of suburban sprawl and preserving the unique qualities of cities. Thus far there is little evidence that urban renewal programs are contributing to those ends. On the contrary, there is considerable evidence to support the argument that government intervention is having the opposite effect.

In order to understand the nature of and the reasons for the failure, it is necessary to review briefly what the function of a city is supposed to be and what makes a city successful. The function can be put in a few words: "Ideally, the unique task of the city is to bring together a multitude of economic and social activities within a limited area, for the enrichment of life by the continued interactions and transactions of varied groups of personalities." [9] As to the characteristics of a city which make it successful in fulfilling this function and attractive to live in, we can discover these by the test of residents' preferences.[10]

[9] Quoted from Lewis Mumford in Catherine Bauer, "Do Americans Hate Cities?" *Journal of the American Institute of Planners*, vol. 23, no. 1 (Winter, 1957), p. 4.
[10] In the following discussion I summarize the findings and argument of Jane Jacobs, *op. cit.*

If we look at the areas in a city where people like to live and spend their time, we find these characteristics: (1) Diversity. Side by side are large apartment houses, small apartment houses, shops, restaurants, theaters, art galleries, and all the other varieties of activities carried on in cities. (2) Interesting streets. The mixture of uses contributes to a continual use of the streets, and the street activity attracts other users who come just to enjoy the scene. (3) Many streets. The streets being the chief attraction, the more successful areas have a larger number of streets and smaller blocks, reducing the dull expanses isolated from street activity. (4) Small scale for pedestrians. The successful urban area is concentrated. It has a minimum of large open expanses, long blank walls, and scattering of buildings which create boring stretches that discourage walking and produce lifelessness.

An area with these characteristics attracts and keeps residents. Because its residents take root, it becomes a cohesive neighborhood and resists blight. Finally, it contributes to the solution of an urban problem, safety. All areas, rural, suburban, and urban, have to face the possibility of crime. Urban concentration may contribute to crime because of the anonymity and "invisibility" that the sheer size of the city confers on the criminal. The city, however, has its own built-in corrective if its streets are in active use. Watching eyes on a busy street are the best guarantee of safety. Hence, an interesting street with a variety of uses that keep it well populated at all hours provides its own protection.

If we turn from examining the successful urban area to what city planners have designed, we find that, far from having learned the lessons of experience, their intent has been to pursue the opposite course. Instead of recognizing population density as one of the ingredients of a good city, planners have set up the goal of decentralization. Instead of diversity, planners have aimed at uniformity—shops concentrated in shopping centers, culture gathered into cultural centers. The lively street has not been accepted as a *sine qua non* of a successful city. Quite the contrary. The street has been treated as something to avoid. Apartment houses are isolated from the street in unused patches of grass. Super-blocks are created to eliminate as many streets as possible. Parking lots and parking garages, elevated highways, blank walls, or vacuous space are introduced which make the streets more boring and discourage walking. The older areas that embody the qualities of a good city are torn down to be "redeveloped" into the planners' dreary dream.

Several reasons can be adduced for these failures of city planning. One is that planners are not permitted to adopt the only solution (even when they recognize it) to the problem of automobiles-and-cities, a destructive mixture. Any attempt to revive the central city by bringing more automobiles into it —more roads, wider streets, bridges, tunnels, speedways, parking spaces—must meet with a twofold failure. More facilities for traffic do not cure traffic congestion. The demand expands to absorb the supply. The chief effects are to make the city a less attractive place to live in and less suited to fulfill its function, and to hasten its disintegration. If successful cities are to be maintained, it can only be by putting a higher price restraint on urban driving or by allowing automobile traffic to throttle itself with its own congestion, and by improving mass public transit facilities to provide speedy transportation into and about the city. Such a solution, however, is plainly unpopular, for the vain hope of reconciling mass automobile transportation with great cities has not yet been laid to rest. The city planners, whatever they may think, have been harnessed to this objective and are assisting in the planned decay of cities.

A second reason for the failure of city planning is that an essential ingredient of a successful city is its *unplanned* quality—its diversity, its mixture of uses, its design and location responding to the preferences of its residents. City planners might undertake to imitate the naturally evolved city; but not only is planned spontaneity difficult to achieve, it raises the question of what planners are needed for.

The customary position in criticizing city planning is that its shortcomings are due to mistaken ideas which can be corrected as they are tried and found wanting. To some extent this view is valid. Many planners have become dissatisfied with their results and have turned back to unplanned cities to see what made them work. Some plans are attempting to incorporate a bit of the diversity of the unplanned city. But the basic contradiction cannot be removed: The planners' function is to impose order on the city; the city, however, needs to evolve in its varied, humanistic disorder.[11]

PRIVATE-ENTERPRISE PLANNING A LA MODE CONTINENTALE

Many of the predominantly private-enterprise countries of Western Europe engage in some sort of exercise which is known as "planning." The general character of this government function can be illustrated with four cases: France, the Netherlands, Sweden, and Norway.

France

French planning [12] consists of drawing up a scheme for resource allocation—investment and output for broad industrial sectors and the government sector, and targets for exports and imports. The actual decisions in these matters, as well as the

[11] The conflict shows up most clearly, of course, in a new city which is entirely planned, like Brasilia. "Seen from the air at night, Brasilia is a diagram of purest white light, shaped like an airplane with a delicate fuselage and curved back-swept wings.

"Once on the ground within the city, however, the beauty of the plan vanishes. . . . The wide, almost empty streets are paved wastes between isolated structures even in the parts of the city that are completed.

"You cannot walk in Brasilia, although most people have to. It is a city planned for beings who are only the manipulating element of a machine. You are staggered by distances between monuments that look beautiful in plan, and which tell architecturally because of their isolation within space, but are remote and cold for the same reason. . . .

"The humanism that people ordinarily bring to a city in spite of everything, breaks through only in pitiful ways in Brasilia. . . ." John Canaday, "Feat or Folly," *The New York Times*, Sept. 17, 1961, p. X 23. It is easy to see what is wrong, but it is difficult to imagine hiring planners to imitate an unplanned city.

[12] See Warren C. Baum, *The French Economy and the State* (Princeton, N.J.: Princeton University Press, 1958); Stanislaw Wellisz, "Economic

subsidiary managerial decisions, are in the hands of the managers of the productive units, including the nationalized enterprises, which are given substantial independence and are operated very much like private enterprises. The chief instrument for implementing the Plan, aside from import restriction, is a degree of financial control over the raising of capital funds, which can be used to discourage investment in some sectors and encourage it in others. This control, however, has weakened considerably since the immediate postwar years, as capital markets have improved and the expansion of internal corporate funds has reduced the need of firms to rely on capital markets. Hence the private sector's adherence to the Plan is, on the whole, voluntary and only approximate.

In the formulation of the Plan, businessmen and technicians of the private sector play a major role as members of specialized advisory commissions. It is probable that the resemblance of Plan and outcome is more owing to the Plan's following the intentions of business than vice versa.

French planning, then, contains very little of what is meant by "central planning," and the French have emphasized the distinction by adopting the descriptive term "indicative planning." Part of the function of indicative planning is to provide information to decision makers, a governmental function in any type of system. In principle, the Plan provides information to each producer about the expected rate of expansion of other sectors and the expected level of demand for his own product. In fact, it seems doubtful that the Plan adds significantly to information received through ordinary trade channels, on which businesses initially based their calculations when they assisted in drawing up the Plan. The Plan figures are, at best, rough indicators of the future. Frequently in the past they have been misleading, or would have been, if followed. For example, un-

---

Planning in the Netherlands, France, and Italy," *Journal of Political Economy*, vol. 68, no. 3 (June, 1960), pp. 252–283; John Sheahan, *Promotion and Control of Industry in Postwar France* (Cambridge, Mass.: Harvard University Press, 1963); Pierre Bauchet, *Economic Planning: The French Experience* (New York: Frederick A. Praeger, Inc., 1964).

derestimates of the rate of technological change have caused under-forecasts of the rate of expansion. At any rate, if the decision makers are left free to use or reject the Plan information, it is unlikely that the Plan will do much harm and it may do some good.[13]

A second function of French indicative planning is to instill in the entrepreneurs the conviction that the economy will continue to grow and thus to sustain in them an expansionist mentality.[14] This psychiatric planning role of inducing entrepreneurs to be enterprising can be understood only in the light of the stagnation that afflicted Europe in the period between the two world wars. For reasons not fully understood,[15] a static vision of the future came to dominate the entrepreneurial mind, with deadening results for investment and innovation. In the postwar period this attitude has clearly been reversed, and producers have been eager to expand and to introduce technological improvements.

What part of the credit for the revival of entrepreneurial buoyancy should be given to the Plan and the "pep rally" features of the planning procedure is in doubt, for the credit must be shared with several other important influences. One of these has been the state of high, and generally excessive, demand in France since World War II. It is certainly doubtful that with-

[13] The reasoning of the child who wrote, "Pins have saved hundreds of lives by the not swallowing of them," is nicely applicable here: Plans have saved dozens of economies by the not following of them. With this insight we can resolve such seemingly contradictory statements as these: "France's indicative planning has contributed to its economic growth. Businessmen have accepted the setting of targets; in fact, they have demonstrated a willingness to increase their own targets [beyond the Plan's] because the environment has proved so encouraging." "U.S. Alters Role in the Economy," *The New York Times*, Apr. 22, 1963.

[14] "French planning is in some important respects the opposite of planning. Knowledge of income and industry projections and faith in the inevitability of expansion are communicated to firms at intra- and inter-industry meetings. This is perhaps the most powerful effect, and one which has a faint resemblance to a revivalist prayer meeting." Charles P. Kindleberger, "The Postwar Resurgence of the French Economy," in Stanley Hoffmann and others, *In Search of France* (Cambridge, Mass.: Harvard University Press, 1963), p. 155.

[15] See Kindleberger, *ibid.*, for discussion of the leading hypotheses.

out the experience of high demand the promises of growth in the Plan would have been persuasive, while the experience of continuous pressure of demand on productive capacity is capable, by itself, of generating an expansionist attitude.

The second factor which contributed to overcoming the stagnationist mentality in France was the shake-up in management personnel and the break-up of old business patterns by the cataclysm of World War II and the German occupation.[16] The encrustation of tradition-bound practices and conservative attitudes, which in other economies is counteracted by the churning of competition, was, in the anti-competitive French setting, effectively shattered by the upheaval of the war.

In addition to "indicative planning," France uses a mixture of price controls, taxes, subsidies, and financial controls which are frequently classified as part of the planning system. The administration of this collection of policy instruments cannot be called "planning" in the sense of a centrally calculated set of coordinated decisions. To a considerable extent these policies are inconsistent and conflicting. For example, some policies are aimed at increasing the scale of firms and eliminating units of inefficient size, while some other policies seek to shelter small business and protect or subsidize inefficient firms. For the most part these government interventions to direct the allocation of resources arise from failure of the price system. This failure in turn arises largely from previous government policies that have distorted prices, interfered with the allocative function of prices, and discouraged competition. When the price system has been so badly damaged, even piecemeal, inconsistent central direction may improve the allocation of resources and be entitled in some loose sense to the name of "planning." Unfortunately, these ". . . makeshift devices of planning made necessary by the absence of realistic prices and monetary equilibrium have . . . come to be regarded as a superior method of economic management by sympathizers of the system." [17]

---

[16] "The economic recovery of France after the war is due to the restaffing of the economy with new men and to new French attitudes." Kindleberger, *ibid.*, p. 156. See also Sheahan, *op. cit.*, p. 9, for a similar view.

[17] Wellisz, *op. cit.*, n. 12, p. 272.

the Netherlands

The Netherlands form of planning represents an even more limited concept than the French.[18] The aims of planning are full employment, stability of the price level, and balance-of-payments equilibrium. The instruments are primarily monetary and fiscal policies. Some control over the general wage level has also been exercised, but this control has been considerably relaxed since 1958. The Plan does not set up production targets or deal with specific projects. In general the economy is operated by free decentralized decision making guided by market forces. Thus, planning in the Netherlands contains no elements of "planning" in the strict sense but is restricted to forecasting macroeconomic variables and utilizing macroeconomic policies for stabilization.

others

Most of the other free-enterprise economies of Western Europe (as well as the United States) can be fitted into either the French or the Dutch category.[19] The Belgian, British, and West German economies, for example, operate on the same principles as the Netherlands. The terminology and the forecasting techniques may differ, the planning ritual may be emphasized less, but the goals of stabilization and balance-of-payments equilibrium and the policy instruments (monetary policy, fiscal policy, and some groping toward a wage policy) are very similar.

When the planning of the free-enterprise countries resembles the French, it is for the same reason: a failure to correct certain obviously correctable disruptions of the price system. In Norway and Sweden, for example, planning of the Dutch

[18] See (Netherlands) Centraal Planbureau, *Scope and Methods of the Central Planning Bureau* (The Hague: August, 1956); C. Weststrate, *Economic Policy in Practice: The Netherlands 1950–1957* (Leiden: H. E. Stenfert Kroese, 1959); Wellisz, *ibid.*

[19] The case of Italy, where the planning effort is primarily directed toward developing the backward economy of southern Italy, belongs among the underdeveloped countries, discussed in the next chapter.

type has been supplemented by controls which allocate investment by economic sector according to a system of priorities.[20] These controls were prompted by the presence of excess investment demand, which distorted the allocative function of the capital market. In both countries, however, it has been generally recognized that the government allocation mechanism is only a crude substitute for a properly functioning capital market. In Sweden, with the gradual elimination of excess demand, controls have been relaxed or eliminated, and planning has shrunk toward a program with pure information and stabilization objectives. In Norway, where the excess demand was greater and where there was considerable reluctance to take strong corrective measures, the trend of planning has been like Sweden's, but at a slower rate.

PUBLIC-ENTERPRISE PLANNING, YUGOSLAV STYLE

The Yugoslav economic organization is a hybrid of decentralized decision making at the enterprise level and centralized investment control at the federal government level, with some semi-decentralized investment decisions by the republican [21] and local governments.[22] The right role for government has been sought by an exploratory and experimental process which is still going on. Government policies in the meantime are highly pragmatic and only vaguely defined in many re-

[20] See Gösta Rehn, "The National Budget and Economic Policy," Skandinaviska Banken *Quarterly Review,* vol. 43, no. 2 (1962), pp. 39–47; Ingvar Svennilson and Rune Beckman, "Long-term Planning in Sweden," *ibid.,* no. 3 (1962), pp. 71–79; Erik Lundberg, "How Successful Has Swedish Stabilisation Policy Been?" *ibid.,* vol. 41, no. 2 (1960), pp. 42–49; Petter Jacob Bjerve, *Planning in Norway, 1947–1956* (Amsterdam: North Holland Publishing Company, 1959).

[21] Yugoslavia is organized as a federation of six republics.

[22] See J. Marcus Fleming and Victor R. Sertic, "The Yugoslav Economic System," International Monetary Fund *Staff Papers,* vol. 9 (July, 1962), pp. 202–205; United Nations, Economic Commission for Europe, *Economic Planning and Management in Yugoslavia,* Economic Bulletin for Europe, vol. 10, 1958; Egon Neuberger, "The Yugoslav Investment Auctions," *Quarterly Journal of Economics,* vol. 73, no. 1 (February, 1959), pp. 88–115.

spects. A description of the Yugoslav government's economic operations must, therefore, be somewhat tentative and limited to broad outlines.

Decisions with regard to type and quantity of production and most other managerial matters are left to the managements of enterprises. Market prices and profitability provide the guidelines for managerial choices. Government intervention in enterprise affairs is mainly concerned with the allocation of investment. Even in that area, the enterprise has considerable freedom, since investment financed with the enterprise's internal funds (retained profits and depreciation allowances) is uncontrolled. However, by its control over borrowed funds and foreign exchange for the import of capital goods, the federal government can exercise considerable influence over the enterprise's total investment program. The investment decision, nevertheless, whether determined by the enterprise or by government, seems to be based primarily on market criteria, much as it would be in a completely decentralized system. Where the investment allocation diverges from the market criteria, it is usually for balance-of-payments reasons; and it takes the form of a preference for investments that will help to earn or conserve foreign exchange, though they may be uneconomic or of low priority by profitability calculations. Other interferences with market allocation of investment may be prompted by distortions of prices which make market calculations inaccurate; although prices are ordinarily set by the market, price fixing and price ceilings are applied sporadically, especially when the economy is under inflationary pressure. Naturally, political and other noneconomic considerations also enter into governmental investment decisions.

Yugoslavia thus provides an interesting example of an economy of publicly owned enterprises (except for modest-sized farms and very small enterprises) operated largely as a decentralized market system. Planning is limited to increasing total investment by restricting consumption and to controlling partially the allocation of investment. Even the controls to allocate investment follow the market, except to the extent that the market is incapacitated by price distortions and inflationary pressures, or to the extent that the political process introduces noneconomic considerations.

THE SOVIET STYLE

To briefly summarize the Soviet system of planning is a troublesome task. The system is complex. It differs significantly in practice from the formal official description, and it is subject to periodic major alterations. The broader outlines, however, are reasonably clear and unchanging, and a sketch of them will be adequate for my purpose.

The first fact to note about Soviet economic planning is that true centralization of decision making has not been attained. The administrative barrier to extreme centralization has been insuperable. Efforts to improve administrative techniques have been more than offset by the growth of the administrative burden as the increasing diversity of products and technical choices has multiplied the information required and the decisions that need to be made. Consequently, several varieties of decentralization have been necessary and have persisted through reorganizations and shiftings between positions of more and less decentralization.

First, a range of important decisions is delegated to the firm or plant manager. (The Plan allocates the materials and capital equipment to each firm, and sets targets for each firm's production, in broad terms of physical units by weight or value.) Within the constraints of materials and capital stock, the manager has considerable freedom of choice. Since it is too cumbersome for the Plan to specify the detailed composition of the targets, the product mix, or composition of the plant's output, is chosen by management. Choices with respect to quality, production techniques, and labor input are also open to management.

A second form of decentralization necessitated by the administrative burden at the center is the division of responsibility among control agencies above the level of the firm. Three different principles enter into the organization of the chain of command: division by industrial sector (for example, textiles, chemicals); division according to function (for example, labor, investment, foreign trade); geographic division into regions. The problem of coordinating decisions among chains of command organized by any one of these principles would impose a very heavy burden on the central administration. The use of all three principles, which evidently cannot be avoided in a scheme of central planning, greatly magnifies the coordination difficulties. The frequent rearrangements of the organizational structure in the Soviet Union have been, in large part, shifts in emphasis or authority among the industrial, functional, and geographic forms of organization.

Once it is recognized that genuine centralization of decision making is impossible, a mechanism for coordinating the behavior of managers and the various control agencies must be sought. This mechanism is conspicuously defective in the Soviet economy. Prices, which normally fulfill this role, are determined not by a market but by government agencies. The prices of inputs bear no dependable relationship to scarcity of those inputs, and the prices of outputs bear no dependable relationship to their relative costs of production or to their utility. Initially the prices are somewhat arbitrary, and they rapidly are made more incorrect by economic change. Calculations based on these prices are recognized to be misleading, with the result that they cannot be permitted to play much part in the allocation of resources. Moreover, one of the operational features of the Soviet system is the maintenance of excess demand and shortages, a condition in which prices cannot perform their allocative function efficiently.

In place of a price system, the central government sets the allocation of materials and production targets for each producing unit. In place of the profit criterion of performance, the Soviet system uses the output test—the fulfillment or surpassing of output targets—supplemented in recent years by the secondary test of cost reduction.

As has been amply demonstrated by economists both outside and inside the Soviet Union,[23] the lack of appropriate prices

[23] See Joseph S. Berliner, *Factory and Manager in the USSR* (Cambridge, Mass.: Harvard University Press, 1957); David Granick, *Management of the Industrial Firm in the USSR* (New York: Columbia Uni-

and of a profit criterion has compelled the use of instructions and motivations which produce economically irrational decisions by managers. In choosing their product mix, managers are more concerned with the test of total output than they are with the optimality of the composition of output. Since the values put on the various products for the purpose of adding up total output do not accurately reflect the value of the output to society, the product mix that the managers choose is frequently markedly inferior. If, for example, the values used for calculation make it easier to meet the plant's target by producing complete assembled units rather than spare parts, the plant will produce insufficient spare parts. A second consequence is the sacrifice of quality for statistical output results. No satisfactory method of balancing the output goal with the cost-reduction goal has been found; priority is ordinarily given to output. The method of controlling production by making certain inputs strategic constraints leads to the managers' treating the others (labor and some materials) as free goods and employing them wastefully. Firms have only limited inducement to adapt output to the demands of their customers; complaints about unresponsiveness of suppliers and shipments of unneeded or useless products are common. The uncertainty of supplies and the lack of a market in which to secure supplies in an emergency lead to the hoarding of excessive inventories and, in many cases, to the uneconomical production of parts within a firm to avoid being placed at the mercy of outside suppliers. The fact that the management can ignore the cost of holding inventories or of producing its own parts encourages these wasteful practices. The enumeration of failings can be continued, but enough has been said to indicate the pervasiveness of the miscalculation and misdirection that must result from the position in which Soviet managers are placed. It is true that outer limits are set on mismanagement by complaints and by the intervention of higher authorities in extreme cases

versity Press, 1954); David Granick, "An Organizational Model of Soviet Industrial Planning," *Journal of Political Economy*, vol. 67, no. 2 (April, 1959), pp. 109–130; Alec Nove, *The Soviet Economy* (New York: Frederick A. Praeger, Inc., 1961); and the Soviet literature cited in these works.

of distorted patterns of production or debased quality, but the scope for inefficiency is still impressive.

Among analysts and practitioners of the Soviet type of planning, all pretense has been abandoned that this method improves on or even approaches the efficiency or rationality of a market system for short-term economic decisions (that is, for allocating an existing supply of inputs). Efforts to improve the mechanism go on, but a resigned acceptance of the inevitable inferiority of the system with respect to short-term management is reflected in the tendency for its proponents to argue that (1) the managerial choices in the operation of enterprises (which loom so large in critiques of the decentralized price system) are really very limited and do not matter much after all; [24] (2) the real importance of planning lies in the making of the long-term or investment decisions; [25] (3) the short-term

[24] See, for example, Maurice Dobb, "A Review of the Discussion Concerning Economic Calculation in a Socialist Economy," in *On Economic Theory and Socialism* (New York: International Publishers Company, Inc., 1955):

"We have seen that an influential argument used in favor of a decentralized mechanism of decision, based on some kind of automatic price-system, is its alleged simplicity, by contrast with an arrangement whereby a complex of choices have to be made by a central authority in face of a highly complex series of alternatives. The force of the argument turns on the actual complexity of the situation with which any group of economic planners is likely to be confronted. Here again it would look as though the abstract model which economists have built has biased their view of reality—in this case the refinement of the model making the problems of economic decision appear actually more cumbrous than they are in cruder reality [p. 81]."

[25] "The sort of efficiency with which the allocation-problem is concerned is the increased effectiveness of resources to be derived from marginal adjustments; this increased effectiveness being confined to those units of resources at the margin which are subject to transfer in the process of moving from an 'imperfect' towards a 'perfect' allocation. The sort of efficiency, by contrast, which comes in the wake of economic development is connected with a rise in the overall effectiveness with which resources in general are used, particularly with a rise in the productivity of labour in consequence of improved organisation, improved technique or more abundant capital equipment (or a conjunction of all three). . . ." *Ibid.*, pp. 79–80.

mismanagement of planning is a small price which must be paid for planning's achievements in long-term growth.[26]

The alleged superiority of centralized investment decisions rests primarily on the supposed reduction of uncertainty under centralization and on the presence of external economies.[27] We have seen that centralization is not in theory expected to decrease primary uncertainty.[28] The reduction of secondary uncertainty through central control depends on whether complete centralization and coordination of decisions can be achieved. The Soviet Union has not been able to approximate complete centralization; sectors or units must still estimate what other sectors or units will do. However, without a consistent set of behavioral rules such as the market provides, it becomes more difficult to predict what others will do, so that secondary uncertainty may well be greater in the Soviet system than in a market system.

The external economies relate chiefly to market interdependence rather than to strictly defined external economies (non-market interdependence).[29] We have seen that the investment problem created by market interdependence is a problem of information and foresight. The argument for the superiority of centralization must hinge on the superiority of the information or foresight available to the planning agency. I have already noted the grounds for doubting that the planner's forecasting is better than or even as good as that of decentralized decision makers in a market economy.

It is difficult to assess so complex a matter as the quality of the Soviet investment pattern, but it can certainly be said that no persuasive testimonial to the achievements of central in-

[26] "In a developing economy, at any rate, there would seem to be little room for doubt that the practical difference between a rapid and a slow rate of increase of productivity, or between a smooth compared with a fluctuating process of growth, can make a difference to welfare that quite dwarfs any claims which an ideal price-mechanism can reasonably make to put the consumer 'further up the hill' of his indifference-map. . . ." *Ibid.*, p. 92.
[27] See pp. 17–18 and 49–51.
[28] See p. 76.
[29] See pp. 16–19.

vestment calculation emerges from it. The decision process has been a combination of imitation of the more advanced economies, efforts to foresee investment requirements, and rectification of errors as they are revealed by disproportions and shortages. Indeed, the Soviet system, which relies heavily on a system of priorities, meeting its critical imbalances by squeezing the low-priority sectors in favor of the high-priority targets, appears to proceed more by response to current data and less by foresight than a private market economy.

In the end we come to the argument that the proof of the pudding is in the growing. Economic growth, provided it is meaningfully defined as the growth of the economy's capacity to add to total satisfaction, while not the sole criterion of economic performance, is a weighty one. If a centralized system is currently less efficient than a market system but can provide a faster rate of growth, the additional production obtained in the long run must eventually compensate for today's waste. We must, therefore, examine the relationship between the Soviet system and its growth achievements.

growth despite planning

Among the commentators on the "success" of the planned systems, the diagnosis of a generation ago has now been stood on its head. The superiority of central calculation over the market has faded from the discussion; the crudities and errors of the calculations relative to the market system, both in the allocation of existing inputs and in the investment choices that determine future allocations, are generally recognized. In so far as one can summarize the current view in one sentence, it is this: The success of the Soviet-type economy lies in its rapid growth which, however, has been achieved in spite of, and not because of, central calculation.[30]

[30] For one example, see Abram Bergson's evaluation of the discussion of irrationality and miscalculation in the Soviet system: "In concentrating on economic efficiency in a static sense, they [Western discussants] tend to neglect the potent economic implications of socialist political control over the rate of investment and technological progress. Through the exercise of its authority in these crucial spheres, the Soviet government has managed to achieve notable economic growth. It achieved

If comprehensive planning hinders rather than helps growth, what are the government functions which do make a contribution to growth? The chief direction of successful government efforts is the acceleration of the rate of capital formation through two channels: the supply of capital and the demand for capital. Keep in mind that I am concerned here only with the advanced or relatively developed economies, which have the institutions and skills that are prerequisite to the productive absorption of a rapidly accelerated flow of investment.

On the supply side, the government can speed capital formation by raising the proportion of national output which is saved.[31] Policies designed to induce a higher rate of private saving are possible, but for a major increase in the aggregate saving ratio, principal reliance must be put on an increase in public saving through a government budgetary surplus.

Augmenting saving is worse than useless unless the demand for investment is correspondingly increased. The opportunity for productive investment, whether the investor is private or public, depends on the demand for output and on the supply of cooperating factors of production combined with the existing technical knowledge. The relation of demand for output to investment opportunity is obvious. The relation of technology and the supply of other inputs to investment is this: In order to put additional capital to productive use, either (1) more labor or more land must be available to combine with the capital according to the techniques now in use, or (2) techniques must be known whereby the existing labor and land can work with more capital.

For all practical purposes, the supply of labor and land may

---

this despite the fact that ruble prices are not especially rational. But granting all this, the fact remains that price distortions are a source of economic waste. If the waste has not been as great as has been assumed, the Soviet experience also testifies that it is not inconsequential." "Comment," in Gregory Grossman (ed.), *Value and Plan* (Berkeley, Calif.: University of California Press, 1960), p. 39. For a forceful presentation of this view, see Peter Wiles, "Growth versus Choice," *Economic Journal*, vol. 66, no. 262 (June, 1956), pp. 244–255.

[31] It is possible that the government can make an additional minor contribution by measures which attract an inflow of foreign capital.

be taken by the government as given. The expansion of technical knowledge, however, does fall within the purview of public policy. It may well be that there is no need for special efforts by the government to expand technical knowledge. This will be the case particularly where the technology in use is far behind the state of technical knowledge already existing, so that there is available, in effect, a great pool of knowledge yet to be drawn upon.[32] Or the growth of knowledge may be adequate without government stimulation to absorb all the additional capital the economy is capable of generating.

In economies where the untapped pool of knowledge is limited, and investment opportunity is being restricted by insufficient innovation potential, a partial solution is available through directing some of the additional investment into the creation of knowledge through education and research. By this means, one type of investment expands the scope for other kinds of investment. The possibilities of this solution should not be exaggerated; investment in the production of knowledge is subject to diminishing returns, just like any other type of investment.[33] Nevertheless, when an economy is underinvesting in knowledge, the correction of this misallocation offers an important means of increasing the growth rate. The government is necessarily involved in this investment decision through its normal function of operating an educational system. The significant question concerns the government's role beyond education. The bulk of technical research will be adequately motivated by market incentives and is not likely to be neglected in private hands. But, as already noted,[34] research, the benefits of which are largely external to the organization paying for it, will be subject to underinvestment unless subsidized or encouraged by either private philanthropy or the government. On the assumption that philanthropy will be in-

---

[32] See Gerald Sirkin, "Economic Growth with Unlimited Supplies of Technical Knowledge," *Economic Weekly*, vol. 15 (Aug. 31, 1963), pp. 1479–1482.

[33] Two limited inputs account for the diminishing returns. One is the supply of creative research talent. The other is the scientific groundwork received from the past, on which current research builds.

[34] See p. 17.

adequate, there remains a strategic role for the government in financing certain types of research.

Finally, taking as given the growth of non-capital inputs and the rate of technical advance, there remains the dependence of the demand for investment on the investors' expectations about the demand for output. No matter how productive the additional units of capital may be, unless the demand for output is expected to expand to absorb the additional product without a fall of price that will erase the advantage of installing more capital, there will be no investment demand. As Kaldor writes,

> It is necessary to postulate a certain minimum "buoyancy" in entrepreneurial behaviour in order to ensure that the investment necessary to generate the profits which call forth a further increase in investment in the next period actually *does* take place, so that productivity, total output, profits and investment continue to grow. Without assuming a certain minimum of "buoyancy," the mere accrual of fresh investment opportunities through technical progress will not alone ensure the continual growth in production —since the latter requires in addition that effective demand and profits should increase sufficiently to match the growth in potential supply, and thus keep the process of accumulation going.[35]

In most private-enterprise economies, the necessary entrepreneurial "buoyancy" is manifest when aggregate demand is near the economy's capacity or when demand has been up to capacity in most of the recent past. But when demand tends to lag behind capacity, entrepreneurial optimism is sapped, and investment demand sags. In some economies, like the French, it is thought that entrepreneurial buoyancy will be lacking even after extended periods of high and expanding demand; hence the program of "indicative planning," intended to reassure entrepreneurs about the future expansion of demand.

[35] "A Model of Economic Growth," *Economic Journal,* vol. 67, no. 268 (December, 1957), pp. 601–602.

Returning now, in the light of these general comments on the role of government in accelerating growth, to the specific case of the Soviet Union, I note six points of particular importance.

1. The Soviet Union started out with a society that was already relatively advanced. I do not mean highly developed; I mean simply not backward in the sense of lacking skills and attitudes which are the prerequisites for economic development.[36] Russia had a long tradition of mathematical, scientific, and engineering study. It had been through a long program of deliberate importation of the technical ideas and attitudes of Western Europe. Though still backward in human resources when compared with England or France, the country nevertheless had a foundation solid enough to permit the "take-off" of the economy after the Reforms of 1861.[37] From 1860 to 1913 the growth rate of industrial output has been estimated at about 5 percent per year and for agricultural output between 1.5 and 2 percent per year.[38] Such growth rates are not remarkable, but they do demonstrate that Russia had established the basis for sustained economic growth before the

[36] See H. Myint, "An Interpretation of Economic Backwardness," *Oxford Economic Papers*, new series, vol. 6, no. 2 (June, 1954), pp.132–163.
[37] See Peter I. Lyashchenko, *History of the National Economy of Russia to the 1917 Revolution* (New York: The Macmillan Company, 1949): "From the preceding discussion we can see the great changes which had occurred in the process of formation of an internal market for industrial capitalism in the course of two or three decades after the Reform of 1861. The general nature of the changes occurring may be summarized as a rapid growth of the social division of labor and commercial farming, a faster tempo in the circulation of goods, and a rise in the domestic demand for production goods for an expanding capitalism, as well as in a demand for articles of personal consumption for the growing cities and their commercial-industrial population [p. 522]." This development laid the foundation for the boom of the 1890s when, "With respect to its tempo of development during these years, Russian industry outstripped nearly all countries [p. 563]." See also Alexander Gerschenkron, "Russia: Patterns and Problems of Economic Development, 1861–1958," in *Economic Backwardness in Historical Perspective* (Cambridge, Mass.: Harvard University Press, 1962).
[38] Raymond W. Goldsmith, "The Economic Growth of Tsarist Russia 1860–1913," *Economic Development and Cultural Change*, vol. 9, no. 3 (April, 1961), pp. 441–475.

Revolution. Hence the Soviet experience is not directly applicable to the development efforts of the backward countries, and comparisons between the growth accomplishments of such countries and the Soviet Union are inappropriate.

2. Throughout the period of Soviet development, the economy has had a supply of redundant labor (labor, mainly in the agricultural sector, which was either openly unemployed or which had negligible productivity). The absorption of this supply of underemployed labor, which has only recently been exhausted, has obviously been an important factor in maintaining a high growth rate.

3. The great technological lag of Russia behind the advanced industrial countries has meant that up to now the rate of technological discovery has not been a constraint on Soviet growth. The Soviet economy has been able to draw on the vast reserves of existing technological knowledge without, in most of the economy, having brought the capital stock to the frontiers of technology where further productive expansion of capital depends crucially on the current rate of advance of technical knowledge.[39]

4. The rapid growth of the capital stock has been made possible by the heavy suppression of consumption and the enforcement of a high saving ratio. This feature of Soviet policy has usually been given the principal credit for the high growth rate, and properly so, provided it is recognized that the efficacy of the high rate of saving is closely related to the social and cultural foundation, the surplus labor, and the surplus technical knowledge mentioned in the preceding three paragraphs. Without those three conditions, so rapid an increase in the

[39] However, the findings of the monumental study by Richard Moorsteen and Raymond P. Powell, *The Soviet Capital Stock, 1928–1962* (Homewood, Ill.: Richard D. Irwin, Inc., 1966), show that despite this potential for rapid technological progress, the Soviet Union's growth of GNP from 1928 to 1961 can be attributed much more to the increased quantity of inputs and much less to the rise of the productivity of inputs than has been the case in the United States. It is difficult to resist the conclusion that, had the Soviet Union concerned itself more with efficiency and good management and less with sheer capital accumulation, it could have achieved the same growth rate in a much less painful way.

capital stock could not have been productively absorbed nor could have yielded the large increase in the rate of growth that it did. Increasing the rate of saving is not a formula for achieving a high rate of growth in all situations.

5. The anticipations of expanding demand which are required to justify producers in expanding their capital stock have been more than adequately provided in the Soviet system. The *shortage system,* a continuous state of demand for output in excess of the capacity of the system, has provided continuous insurance that management's demand for additional capital exceeds the economy's ability to provide it. However, the Soviet economy has paid a great price for this high-pressure method. A state of chronic shortage gives rise to many forms of uneconomic behavior: hoarding of inventories, production within plants of supplies which could be more economically produced elsewhere, insufficient quality control, and so on. It is by no means clear that the Soviet Union's excess demand was a desirable element in its growth program. There is abundant evidence from other economies that a rising level of demand, kept near but not in excess of the economy's capacity, is sufficient to generate the necessary entrepreneurial buoyancy for capital expansion, while the inefficiencies associated with excess demand detract from the rate of growth. The best one can say for excess demand is that it is advantageous to growth if the alternative is a deficiency of demand.

6. Totalitarian control is frequently credited with making an important contribution to rapid growth in the Soviet Union. What is meant by this proposition is that the preferences of individuals seriously conflict with the objective of growth and that the suppression of individual choice can accelerate growth.

The area of conflict between individual choice and growth can easily be exaggerated. In many respects, especially in management and research, the two are positively related. Likewise, the gains in growth through suppression of individual freedom can be greatly overestimated. Even in the most tightly controlled society which does not scruple to use the techniques of terror, the power to regulate individual behavior encounters surprising limitations. Fainsod's description of bureaucratic self-protection against authoritarianism could be applied at all levels of society:

> The insecurity developed by these arrangements engenders its own antidotes. In order to escape the heavy burden of distrust which the system imposes on those who are involved in it, both controlled and controllers not infrequently cover up for each other's sins and omissions in discharging the tasks for which they are held jointly responsible. The urge to find a peaceful sanctuary is deepseated among Soviet administrators and it comes into sharp conflict with the Hobbesian war of all against all upon which the ruling group relies in order to maintain its control and security. The literature of Soviet administration is filled with criticisms of administrators who enter into so-called family relations with each other and with the control organs that surround them. Despite the virulence of the denunciations, the phenomenon is recurrent, and it apparently registers a strongly felt need to erect barricades against the intrusive checks used by the regime to maintain the pressure of its power. . . .[40]

At levels below the bureaucracy it is undoubtedly even more difficult to exercise control and to force changes in the patterns of behavior. A combination of positive incentives and indoctrination is usually found in the end to offer a faster route to harnessing individual motivations to the goal of economic expansion than the use of authoritarian direction. As Nove says:

> The role of terror in this context is widely misunderstood. It was very largely of negative value—it suppressed opposition, and made possible rapid capital accumulation by the imposition of sacrifices. While it certainly facilitated through forced labor, as a by-product of mass arrests, the development of remote and inhospitable regions, the immense economic waste—including the killing off of scarce

[40] Merle Fainsod, *How Russia Is Ruled*, rev. ed. (Cambridge, Mass.: Harvard University Press, 1963), pp. 388–389.

technicians and administrators—make it (in my view) absurd to assert that the material achievements of the Soviet regime were directly attributable to terror and forced labor. Thus it is no coincidence that the economic sector in which coercion played the greatest role—collective agriculture—remained the most backward; orders unrelated to self-interest could not be translated into effective action. In any event, few can doubt that the complex and increasingly educated Soviet society of today cannot function efficiently without a much greater degree of voluntary cooperation "below." The post-Stalin period in the USSR has been characterized by efforts to find some way of reconciling the political power of the party with the need to secure more active participation among the citizens. The interpretation which insists on "pure totalitarian power" cannot explain the major concessions which have in fact been made.[41]

The sheer power to order people about, then, is more likely to retard than to assist the growth process. It generates resistance and evasion, fails to enlist cooperation, discourages initiative, stifles experimentation by increasing the risks of deviating from prescribed patterns, and increases the likelihood of error by suppressing open discussion and criticism.

We come nearer the truth if we say that the political basis of a successful economy is not totalitarian government but *strong* government. Specifically, the government must be strong enough to resist the many claims for special treatment and demands for government intervention on behalf of particular interests. Strong government does not mean unresponsive government, but government secure enough to be unresponsive to demands that sacrifice the general economic welfare for special interests.

The question of strong government, in its relation to economic growth, becomes particularly acute when the government undertakes to restrict consumption and increase aggregate saving. Let us assume that conditions are such that a sub-

[41] Alec Nove, *Communist Economic Strategy: Soviet Growth and Capabilities* (Washington, D.C.: National Planning Association, 1959), pp. 5–6.

stantial increase in saving will yield a substantial increase in the rate of growth. Let us further assume that general agreement could be obtained that current sacrifices of consumption and faster growth would increase the general welfare. Nevertheless, a weak government may find that it lacks the taxing power to impose the desired restraints on consumption. The greater the intended suppression of consumption, the stronger the government must be, until strong government verges on totalitarian government. In the case of the Soviet Union, the extreme reduction of living standards, especially in the agricultural sector, which the government sought could have been accomplished only by totalitarian methods. The ruthless restriction of consumption was, as Nove suggests in the quotation above, the only positive contribution of totalitarianism to rapid growth.

In the light of this discussion of the foundations of Soviet growth, we can now ask how impressive the Soviet achievements in growth actually have been. Measuring economic growth involves the familiar difficulties of the choice of the best indicator, statistical accuracy, index-number problems, and the selection of an appropriate time period. Sovietologists in the United States, using gross national product as the indicator, calculate the average Soviet growth rate at 6.7 percent per year for the period 1950–1960. From 1960 to 1964, they calculate that the rate fell to 5.5 percent.[42]

These estimates, despite the great care with which the statistical analysis was carried out, overstate the progress of the Soviet economy. Statisticians are unable to adjust for what Michael Polanyi has called "conspicuous production" [43]—production which adds more to statistics than to welfare. When buyers are given wide choice, and when their choices help to determine prices, the relative prices serve to measure the value of additions to output. But when choice is restricted, when buyers have little influence on the composition of output, and when

[42] Stanley H. Cohn, "Soviet Growth Retardation: Trends in Resource Availability and Efficiency," in U.S. Congress, Joint Economic Committee, *New Directions in the Soviet Economy, part II-A, Economic Performance,* 1966, table 2, p. 105.

[43] "Towards a Theory of Conspicuous Production," *Soviet Survey,* no. 34 (October–December, 1960), pp. 90–99.

there is continual shortage and rationing, prices become meaningless as gauges of relative values. Statistics then measure physical product, not value, and a 10 percent increase of physical product does not necessarily increase value by 10 percent. For example, a million suits, all the same color and style, will not provide the same value as the same number of suits of identical quality which cater to the consumers' desire for choice of color and style. To the extent that the Soviet economy gives priority to planners' over consumers' preferences, that it narrows the range of choice relative to what consumers would be willing to pay for, and that it imposes delays, uncertainty, and other inconveniences, the statistical estimates of output overstate the true rate of economic improvement.

Nevertheless, for the sake of discussion let us use the gross national product growth estimates as a measure of Soviet economic progress. Is that growth a remarkable achievement and a tribute to central economic control? Only a comparison between countries broadly similar in their potential for growth and differing in the economic policies of their governments can shed light on this question. As previously noted, the Soviet Union had three major bases for potential growth: the long ascent before the Revolution from backwardness to modern industrial skills and institutions, great reserves of underused manpower, and great reserves of unused technical knowledge. To this the government added totalitarian control, planning, and the enforcement of a high rate of saving. It is not easy to find another country that offers an illuminating comparison. Obviously not much is to be learned by comparing the growth rates of the U.S.S.R. and the United States, which always had a labor scarcity and always was in the forefront in the application of technical knowledge. For a suitable comparison with the Soviet Union, I can think only of the case of Japan.

Japan began its campaign against backwardness after the Meiji Restoration in 1868, at approximately the same time as the beginning of Russia's drive toward modernization after the Reform of 1861. The Japanese, however, started from a more backward position, for their previous contact with the advanced industrial societies had been meager compared with Russia's.

Japan, like the Soviet Union, has had large reserves of labor and could draw upon the great pool of technical knowledge provided by the advanced countries. It also has tended to save a high proportion of total income, relative to most countries. Where Japan and the Soviet Union have chiefly differed has been in the economic role of the government. The Japanese economy has been essentially a private-enterprise system, and the economic functions of government have been those which are the responsibility of government in any system plus those policies which encourage enterprise and improve the working of the market system.[44]

The Japanese gross national product grew, from 1950 to 1960, at an average rate of 8 percent per year. From 1960 to 1964 the average growth rate rose to 11 percent per year.[45] Those given to drawing bold conclusions from growth data would have to conclude from this comparison that, given a developed institutional base and large reserves of unemployed labor and technology, impressive rates of growth can be achieved through high rates of saving in either a free-enterprise or a planned economy, but that the free-enterprise economy will do somewhat better. It may be objected that Japan is a special case. Certainly it is. The Soviet Union is also a special case. The point is that they are both special in precisely those respects that make a comparison of their growth rates meaningful.

[44] See William Lockwood, *The Economic Development of Japan: Growth and Structural Change, 1868–1938* (Princeton, N.J.: Princeton University Press, 1954). "Yet the picture which emerges does not show the State in the central planning and directing role often ascribed to it, so far as the principal areas of economic growth are concerned. Especially is this true of the period after 1890, when the great expansion took place. . . . The truly signal contributions to economic growth which were made through the political mechanism were, first, to ward off foreign subjection and assure the nation's political unity and order; second, to clear away the whole complex of legal and political obstacles to freedom of ownership, occupation, and movement; and third, to carry through a series of architectural reforms in law, education, taxation, currency, etc. which created a setting favorable to the emergence of new forms of productive enterprise [p. 588]. . . ."
[45] Stanley H. Cohn, *op. cit.*

113

6 | government in backward and underdeveloped economies

In the literature on economic development, a special and enlarged economic role is ordinarily assigned to the government in underdeveloped areas. This chapter reexamines the characteristics of such areas which bear on the question of the government's economic function and the case for and against specific types of intervention.

BACKWARDNESS AND UNDERDEVELOPMENT

The areas commonly designated as "underdeveloped" can be better understood if we distinguish among them according to their degree of backwardness.[1] By *backwardness* I mean a deficiency in the population of certain characteristics which are necessary for the creation and operation of a complex, changing, and expanding economy. A "backward" society and its inhabitants may be quite advanced in other respects like culture or manners; I am concerned here only with backwardness in the qualities that are prerequisites for economic development.

Among the deficiencies in a backward society are

[1] See H. Myint, "An Interpretation of Economic Backwardness," *Oxford Economic Papers*, new series, vol. 6, no. 2 (June, 1954), pp. 132–163.

those of mechanical, scientific, and administrative skills, and of certain attitudes, including discipline and responsibility, cooperativeness, and receptivity to change. The extent of the deficiency in the preconditions for development varies widely. There is no clear demarcation between backward and advanced societies. Nevertheless, one can say that some countries are so lacking in the requisite qualities that no significant economic development can take place, and in others, though economic improvement is occurring, the chief developmental task remains the overcoming of backwardness.

An *underdeveloped* but not backward country is one which, though it has an adequate groundwork in terms of the skills and attitudes of its people, has not proceeded very far in the modernization of its economy through the accumulation of capital and the use of the more capital-intensive techniques or the production of the more capital-intensive products that are suitable to its resources and markets. Russia and Japan at the turn of the century, Israel and Mexico today, will serve to illustrate the type.

The functions of the government in promoting economic development will obviously differ sharply in backward economies and in underdeveloped, non-backward economies. First, the order of priorities of government efforts must differ. In the backward economy, achieving the preconditions for development must take precedence, since efforts at development inevitably go to waste when they are imposed on people unequipped or unwilling to introduce economic improvements. Second, the capability of the government sets a narrower limit in a backward society on the functions which the government can appropriately assume. The same shortcomings of skills and attitudes that impede economic development also disable the government as an initiator and "implementor" of extensive and complex development programs. In an underdeveloped economy, where backwardness is no longer a major obstacle, the capabilities of government administration are increased, but, at the same time, the importance and scope of the government functions in the economy are reduced.

In an examination of the economic role of the government in backward and underdeveloped economies, it is unnecessary to repeat the list of standard government functions which are generally accepted as the legitimate and essential business of government in any type of economy.[2] The question to be considered here is whether the nature of these economies creates a need for different or more extensive government intervention than in an advanced economy.

THE ATTACK ON BACKWARDNESS

In any society which is agreed on the objective of economic development, the necessity and desirability of government efforts to introduce the skills and attitudes necessary for development cannot be denied. Exactly how the government goes about this, however, is far from clear.

The answer is simple enough when we are dealing with those qualities that can be transmitted by formal education. The establishment of a school system is, by this time, standard government procedure. The vastly more difficult task is to change the attitudes and customs which block development. Indeed, without that change, formal schooling will largely go to waste. A common experience in backward societies has been that literacy evaporates when schooling is finished, because an interest in or a sense of the need for reading ability has not been developed. The inclination of backward societies is to regard education as a symbol of status rather than a useful tool, with the result that formal education produces mainly people who regard themselves as above farming or other manual labor. This attitude, while consistent with the training of an elite, is a serious obstacle to the achievement of the skilled agricultural and industrial labor force which is required for rapid technological advancement.

The list of attitudes, customs, and social institutions which impede economic development is long and differs from country to country. It includes resistance to change of techniques, products, or occupations; irresponsibility, unreliability, and a general unconcern for efficiency; strong distrust of "outsiders"

[2] See Chap. 2 above, pp. 8–9.

(those outside the family or close-knit community); a deficient capacity for cooperation and compromise; immobility of factors because of social compartmentalization along caste, class, regional, or other lines; social arrangements which prevent the most able from rising to positions of leadership or which discourage individual initiative; a deficiency of the inquisitive, questioning, experimenting mentality which provides the basis for scientific work.[3]

Overcoming these forms of backwardness is at best a slow process, a matter of decades, not years. What the government can do to accelerate the process is still uncertain. Programs of indoctrination, persuasion, demonstrations, subsidies, increased contact between the backward and more advanced areas, and school education, can make inroads on the traditional mores and institutions. However, too much hope should not be pinned on governments as agents of rapid social change, for they operate under several severe handicaps.

The essential shortcomings of all governments as decision makers (outlined in Chapter 4) are magnified in a backward society, since the same backwardness that hinders rational action in the economic sphere hinders it in the governmental sphere.

A second handicap under which governments labor in backward societies is the popular attitude toward government. In an atmosphere generally pervaded by suspicion, the most suspect of all is the government. There are, of course, good historical reasons for this mistrust of government; but whether currently merited or not, it weakens the capacity of the government to persuade or enlist the cooperation of its citizens. Winning the public's confidence thus becomes a prior requirement for much of the government's effort to modernize social behavior. Excessive government zeal for modernization in the early stages only

[3] For an extended discussion, see W. Arthur Lewis, *The Theory of Economic Growth* (London: George Allen & Unwin, Ltd., 1955), chaps. 2, 3.

Interesting insights are provided by Edward C. Banfield, *The Moral Basis of a Backward Society* (Glencoe, Ill.: The Free Press, 1962) and Everett E. Hagen, *On the Theory of Social Change* (Homewood, Ill.: Dorsey Press, Inc., 1962).

increases the alienation of the public from its government and reduces the effectiveness of the program for change.

The third and most serious of the difficulties that may be encountered by a campaign against backwardness frequently arises from a conflict of objectives. The government may seek rapid modification of social attitudes and arrangements and, at the same time, be unwilling to permit a competitive market system to operate freely. Yet a free market is a powerful instrument for the rapid establishment of the social basis for economic development. A competitive market is a strict disciplinarian, compelling resource mobility, opening channels for the rise of the able and ejecting the incompetent, forcing technical change, and enforcing discipline in the labor force. Such a reconstruction of the society is not pleasant to live through, and we may expect that ordinarily a far larger portion of the citizenry will oppose it than will applaud it. Thus a popular government which maintains extensive control of the economy will find it difficult to promote or even allow those social changes which the market can carry out if permitted. The third alternative to either the paternal popular government or market discipline is the totalitarian government. The instrument for rapid social modernization, then, is either the free market or totalitarianism, while the "middle way," seeking to dispense with both the market and the cruelties and blunders of authoritarian rule, must forego the objective of speed.

entrepreneurship

A particularly crucial aspect of backwardness, one on which a great deal of the case for government intervention in underdeveloped economies has been built, is the alleged shortage of entrepreneurship. Entrepreneurship is a blend of certain personality traits and administrative capabilities which enable a man to visualize new opportunities, to initiate and carry through the organization of an enterprise, and to seek to vitalize the enterprise by the continuous introduction of improvements.

As far as the requisite personality traits are concerned—

119

venturesomeness, independence, determination, and so on—they occur with adequate frequency in any society. What is often lacking is an environment in which latent entrepreneurial talent can flourish. As Lewis observes,

> In every community there are some men whose natural bent is to experiment with new techniques, new products or new economic forms, in defiance of established opinion or of vested interests. Some societies admire and encourage such people, while others regard them as buccaneers to be suppressed, but economic growth depends very largely on the extent to which the social atmosphere nourishes such people and gives them scope.[4]

The training of potential entrepreneurs to develop the necessary organizational and administrative skills can be assisted to only a minor extent by school programs. The acquisition of some managerial techniques can be accelerated by formal business and administrative training, but the bulk of the entrepreneur's education must come from experience in operating an enterprise. Hence the supply of able entrepreneurs is increased fastest in a system which offers the greatest opportunity for potential entrepreneurs to gain experience in independent decision making (in a system of many decentralized productive units).

The shortage of entrepreneurs in backward economies is frequently given as a major reason for government initiation and operation of enterprises. The argument is faulty on several counts: (1) The scarcity of entrepreneurs is somewhat exaggerated in a number of countries. What is severely limited in many countries is not the supply of entrepreneurs, but the opportunity to exercise entrepreneurship. The limitation may be due to overt governmental restriction or it may be due to the failure of government to perform its ordinary functions (maintenance of law and order, communications, monetary and fiscal policy, etc.) in a way which creates an encouraging atmosphere for entrepreneurship. (2) Public enterprise requires entrepreneurship no less than private enterprise. A true short-

[4] Lewis, *op. cit.*, p. 51.

age of entrepreneurs will not be corrected by organizing production under government rather than private auspices. The sole difference is that the public entrepreneur may receive from the government the cooperation that is denied to the private entrepreneur. (3) The production of more and better entrepreneurs is retarded by government control of productive enterprises, since the centralization of decision making and the limitations on the entry of new firms curtail the breeding grounds of entrepreneurship.

A somewhat different argument for public entrepreneurship rests, not on the shortage of entrepreneurs, but on the paralyzing effect of high risk on private entrepreneurship in underdeveloped economies. Risks are generally higher in these new and untried situations; on the other hand, so are the possible gains. It is not clear that, given the opportunity and incentive, private entrepreneurship will not undertake to invest up to the limit set by the supply of other inputs and the size of the market. Nor is it clear that the use of public enterprise is the surest or most satisfactory way to meet the problem of risk. Unless the public decision makers are to be held responsible in some significant way for their decisions, the cost of risk will be omitted from their calculations, and the calculations will be erroneous. The alternative (and typical) method is to make government officials bear part of the risk through potential political defeat or loss of positions in the bureaucracy. In that case, the system is again confronted with the possibility of extreme risk aversion. The chief difference from private entrepreneurship is that the *rewards* of risk bearing do not accrue to the public entrepreneur, and therefore the inducements to take the risks which they should take are inadequate.

The only really satisfactory approach to the risk barrier is a direct attempt to reduce risk. Governments which provide equitable treatment of enterprise, adequate credit facilities, and a generally encouraging climate for investment have not found entrepreneurship to be a bottleneck. Where governments begin with a preference for public enterprise, where they add to the risk of private enterprise, and where they provide funds for public enterprise on terms and in amounts greatly superior to what is available to private enterprise, a weakness of private entrepreneurial effort will, not surprisingly, be found.

land reform and entrepreneurship

Land reform, in the sense of converting tenant farmers into owner farmers, though partially inspired by egalitarianism, derives strong support from the proposition that it will raise agricultural productivity. The transfer of landownership from absentee holders to those working the land is expected to encourage the improvement of land and the introduction of better techniques and to increase the incentive to accumulate capital and expand output.[5] This type of land reform, then, is one facet of the general program to improve entrepreneurship. Redistribution of land will not necessarily improve entrepreneurship in all forms of agriculture, but where it will, land reform is part of the attack on backwardness.

population control

Another feature of backwardness under present conditions of falling mortality rates is the population explosion. Basically the problem comes down to the fact that modernization of a society operates more slowly in reducing the birth rate than in reducing the death rate. The resulting rise in the rate of population growth retards or prevents a rise in the standard of living, hinders development, and generates acute stresses and frustrations which threaten political and social stability. The problem is somewhat less severe in a country which has reserves of unused land, but this mitigating factor secures only a short-term postponement of the full impact of a high rate of population growth. Government programs to correct the backwardness that sustains high birth rates is, therefore, an essential part of the development effort. Unfortunately, high birth rates are only a symptom of the general state of the society's attitudes, and progress in introducing family limitation can proceed scarcely any faster than the modernizing of the culture.

[5] See Philip M. Raup, "The Contribution of Land Reforms to Agricultural Development: An Analytical Framework," *Economic Development and Cultural Change*, vol. 12, no. 1 (October, 1963), pp. 1–21.

THE ATTACK ON UNDERDEVELOPMENT

An underdeveloped economy is one in which the techniques of production and the range of products lag markedly behind the techniques and products which are known and suitable to the nation's population and natural resources. Since all economies have room for improvement in their techniques and composition of products, "underdevelopment" is obviously a relative term.

The chief obstacle to development is backwardness. This is true by definition, since backwardness has been defined as the characteristics of the society and people that give rise to forms of behavior which are hostile to the adoption of new techniques and products. Nevertheless the tautology is useful in reminding us that, in an uncongenial environment, the mechanics of development—pumping in capital and borrowed technology—have met with and will meet with but limited success. It does not follow that efforts at development must be postponed until some critical stage in the remaking of society is reached. The introduction of new industries and experiments in new techniques, even if their direct contribution to growth is minor, are ways of shaking up a traditionalist society and thereby speeding change. But there are limits set by the social environment to the rate at which capital and technology can be absorbed. Conversely, once the soil has been properly prepared, the capacity to fruitfully plant capital and new technology greatly expands, and the bottleneck of development becomes the rate of capital formation.

accelerating capital formation

The least painful method of accelerating capital formation is to draw upon foreign saving, either from private sources or through grants and loans from foreign governments and international agencies. The preference of the borrowing country will ordinarily be for funds from governmental sources or international agencies, provided no objectionable strings are attached, since the cost of these funds is nil or below the market rate. However, the supply of such funds is small relative to the capital needs of the underdeveloped countries, and there is little a recipient country can do to expand its share beyond establishing its capacity to use the capital productively. The flow of capital from foreign private sources is also quite limited, in large part because of the comparative risk to the lenders. Even with the best efforts to create a favorable climate for foreign investment, it is doubtful that the inherent risks can be much reduced. In any event, limits to the developed countries' supply of savings in excess of the amount they will tend to absorb at home put a tight constraint on the potential foreign borrowing by the underdeveloped world.

The mere quantity of foreign capital, however, does not fully reflect its contribution to development. Foreign capital provides not only saving but *foreign exchange*. In other words, foreign capital provides, as domestic saving cannot,[6] access to the equipment and materials of other countries. Under the generally prevailing conditions of foreign-exchange shortage in underdeveloped countries, there is a serious bottleneck in importing inputs, which restricts the rate of capital formation. When foreign exchange is a constraint, foreign capital permits investment, not only of the resources obtained abroad, but also of the domestic resources which require foreign equipment to combine with and which could not be put into capital formation otherwise. In addition, foreign capital, especially in the case of direct investment by businesses, frequently brings with it technical assistance and administration which are extremely valuable in the initial stages of new projects.

The chief source of capital accumulation must ordinarily be domestic saving. The rationale for government intervention in the rate of saving for the purpose of affecting the rate of capital accumulation has already been examined.[7] As we have seen, the need for government adjustment of the rate of saving will tend to be comparatively slight in advanced countries, but

[6] In principle, domestic saving, by making available an "exportable surplus," can also provide foreign exchange. In practice, the export difficulties of the underdeveloped countries prevent any ready conversion of domestic saving into foreign exchange.

[7] See "Optimizing the Rate of Saving," Chap. 2 above, pp. 31–32.

in a newly developing economy the case may be quite different. In an advanced country, where the latest technological knowledge is being applied, the contribution to growth which an increase in the rate of saving can make will be rather small. In an underdeveloped economy, on the other hand, the case for public measures to increase the total saving ratio may be considerably stronger.

An underdeveloped economy, being able to draw upon the accumulated technological knowledge of the developed economies, is in a position to add substantially to the rate of growth by increasing the saving ratio. The increase in the growth rate will be even greater if the economy has a large amount of labor which is structurally unemployed because of insufficient capital. It is true that the private returns to saving will, in this situation, be greater than in a developed economy, and the private motivation to save will be correspondingly stronger. Nevertheless, the larger the contribution which increased saving can make to the growth rate, the greater the significance that attaches to the external returns to saving and the greater the probability that government intervention to raise the aggregate saving ratio will bring the society closer to an optimum saving position. Obviously it is possible to carry the saving program beyond the optimal point: Where governments are acutely unresponsive to individual preferences, it is not unlikely that excessive sacrifices will be imposed for accelerated capital accumulation. It should be further noted that the case for publicly augmenting saving applies with much less force in backward societies, where the capacity to absorb additional capital is still limited by the nature of their skills and institutions.

balanced growth

The ideas which most generally underlie the support for planning in underdeveloped economies can be grouped under the heading of "balanced growth." [8] The balanced-growth argument, briefly summarized, is this:

[8] An early presentation of the essence of the argument is P. N. Rosenstein-Rodan, "Problems of Industrialisation of Eastern and South-eastern

1 Producers' investment decisions are interdependent because the expansion of a firm in one industry creates demand in other industries. The individual entrepreneur, if he knows that other industries are expanding, knows that his own market will be expanding, and has an inducement to invest in additional productive capacity. On the other hand, the entrepreneur who has no knowledge that other entrepreneurs intend to expand underestimates the growth of his market and is discouraged from investing.

2 Producers' investment decisions are interdependent because one firm's expansion is dependent on the supply of certain inputs produced by other firms. An entrepreneur not knowing that his suppliers intend to expand will himself hesitate to expand.

3 Because the profitability of each firm's investment is affected through these demand-and-supply interdependencies by the investment of other firms, decentralized investment decisions will result in low rates of investment and growth. Each firm waits for the others to expand. Centralized decision making, on the other hand, could break through the impasse by coordinated investment programs.

In the face of such difficulties, one may wonder how to account for the long history of successful expansion of the many countries that have decentralized investment decision

Europe," *Economic Journal,* vol. 53, no. 210–211 (June–September, 1943), pp. 202–211. See also Ragnar Nurkse, *Problems of Capital Formation in Underdeveloped Countries* (Oxford: Basil Blackwell, 1953).

Tibor Scitovsky, "Two Concepts of External Economies," *Journal of Political Economy,* vol. 62, no. 2 (April, 1954), pp. 143–151, is an analysis of the theoretical base. For a critique of some of the balanced-growth ideas, see John Sheahan, "International Specialization and the Concept of Balanced Growth," *Quarterly Journal of Economics,* vol. 72, no. 2 (May, 1958), pp. 183–197; Paul Streeten, "Unbalanced Growth," *Oxford Economic Papers,* new series, vol. 11, no. 2 (June, 1959), pp. 167–190.

making. It is fairly obvious that entrepreneurs are not paralyzed by decentralization. What in fact happens is that some entrepreneurs believe it profitable to expand even without expectations of general economic growth. They thereby increase the demand of other entrepreneurs, who are then induced to invest. The original expansionists find their optimism thus justified and expand further. Entrepreneurs learn to anticipate the growth of demand that will validate their own expansion, and they learn to expect that their suppliers will react to demand so that the supplies needed for expansion will be forthcoming. Decentralization is no preventer of growth, given only a certain minimal venturesomeness and a responsiveness by entrepreneurs to the opportunities created.

The usual balanced-growth criticism of decentralization is not that decentralization entirely prevents growth, but that it retards it. In Rosenstein-Rodan's terms, decentralization increases the risk of investment because of doubts about being able to sell additional output.[9] I have already noted that this type of risk—secondary risk—can be reduced by improving information for entrepreneurs about the intentions of other entrepreneurs.[10] Centralized decision making is only one way of improving the information, and it is not necessarily the best way. Because of uncertainty about the principles on which government decisions will be made, it is frequently more difficult to forecast the investment requirements of any particular product in a centralized-decision economy than in a market economy. The government's chief contribution to reducing secondary risk is through giving reasonable assurance that aggregate demand will expand with the economy's capacity. That assurance, however, can be given through the government's macroeconomic instruments of monetary and fiscal policy. With high and expanding aggregate demand underwritten by macroeconomic policy, the risk to one expanding entrepreneur that the rest of the economy will not also expand

---

[9] "The planned creation of such a complementary system reduces the risk of not being able to sell, and, since risk can be considered as a cost, it reduces cost. It is in this sense a special case of 'external economies.'" Rosenstein-Rodan, *ibid.*, p. 206.

[10] See pp. 18–19.

becomes slight, and the need for the centralization of investment decisions to reduce risk evaporates.

Upon close examination, the argument that in underdeveloped countries decentralized investment decision making stifles investment reduces to the proposition that there is a lack of entrepreneurship. "A hesitant investor," says one proponent of centralization, wants more than information; he wants "a *guarantee* that complementary industries are to be established. . . ." [11] A country so lacking in the enterprising spirit would, no doubt, have difficulty in generating investment in a decentralized economy; it would have much the same difficulty under centralization, where entrepreneurship is no less necessary.

Onto the original balanced-growth proposition—that investment decisions must be centralized so as to provide the assurance to each productive unit that the demand for its additional output and the supplies of its additional input requirements will be forthcoming—there has been grafted an allied proposition: that planning must provide for diversified investment so that the various industries will grow simultaneously according to some balanced pattern prescribed by the linkages of demand and supply among them. Actually, there is no technical necessity for simultaneous expansion of industries according to a fixed pattern. A part of the economy can be expanded faster than the industries to which it is linked backward for its supplies or forward to its customers. The disequilibrium which is thus created exerts pressure on the suppliers to expand and creates inducements for the customers to expand.[12]

The disequilibrium introduced by "unbalanced growth," as a

---

[11] S. K. Nath, "The Theory of Balanced Growth," *Oxford Economic Papers*, new series, vol. 14, no. 2 (June, 1962), p. 143.

[12] An "unbalanced" pattern of expansion does not necessarily mean that the economy is in disequilibrium. In an economy which can engage in international trade, some degree of specialization is optimal. A disequilibrium resulting from unbalanced growth must refer to a maladjustment in the structure of production after allowance for the pattern of international trade.

recent study [13] has pointed out, will be an advantage rather than a drawback under the conditions generally prevailing in underdeveloped countries. In any society, there will be some tendency to postpone decisions and to lag in implementing them. The tendency to wait and see, to study the matter further, to call another conference, is ever present. Moreover, where interests conflict, contending forces can drag out the process of arriving at a decision. In an underdeveloped economy the difficulties of decision making are greatly intensified. The decisions which must be made often represent a major break with the past and cannot be well grounded in experience; reliable information is scarcer than in developed countries, decision-making talent is scarce, tradition is still a binding force, administration is still geared to the ancient objective of avoiding responsibility, and the conflicting interests that are aroused in the attempt at extensive remodeling of the society are particularly liable to frustrate action.

In the face of this propensity to inaction, the disequilibrium of unbalanced growth has the great virtue of exerting pressure on decision makers through the shortages and distortions it creates. The delays and obstructions eventually give way before the compelling need to correct the disequilibrium. "If the economy is to be kept moving ahead, the task of development policy is to maintain tensions, disproportions, and disequilibria." [14]

Keeping in mind that balanced-growth proposals require government planning and implementation, we should note that the government sector is the part of the economy which suffers most acutely from the turgidity of the decision process. The lack of competition, the inadequacy of rewards for risk taking, the preference for risk avoidance in government bureaucracy, and the use of the political process by opposed social interests to frustrate each other, all help to account for this. The notion of propelling the economy forward by government direction of some pattern of balanced expansion, is, therefore, unrealistic.

[13] Albert O. Hirschman, *The Strategy of Economic Development* (New Haven, Conn.: Yale University Press, 1958).
[14] *Ibid.*, p. 66.

A realistic version is one in which unbalanced growth, creating distortions and crises, propels the government forward to expand transportation, power, or whatever other sector has been entrusted to it.

In a world with no impediments to the free flow of correct decisions, with extensive economic information available at little cost, and with excellent forecasting, an optimum pattern of expansion in continuous equilibrium might be a reasonable objective. This optimum pattern, however, would not necessarily be highly diversified. Its shape would be dictated by economies of scale, the possibilities for international trade, and the substitutability among inputs and among outputs. The notion of an antithesis between balanced growth and specialization is one of the erroneous outgrowths of the balanced-growth discussion.

In the world as we know it, continuous equilibrium is impossible. Nor should we want it, considering the forward impetus which unbalanced growth supplies. The curious and unfortunate outcome in economies that bind themselves to a detailed plan for expansion is that, while they cannot prevent the distortions that result from imperfect foresight, imperfect information, delays, and inaction, they deaden the normal reactions to the distortions by the rigidity of the plan. Thus, they have the disequilibrium, but they manage to dissipate its potential usefulness.

LIMITATIONS OF GOVERNMENT

It is unnecessary to review all the factors previously discussed which limit a government's capacity to improve the working of an economy. They apply in underdeveloped as well as in developed countries. But it is necessary to emphasize that many of the limitations will be more acutely felt in underdeveloped countries, where expectations about what the government can accomplish soar higher, and governmental capacities are lower, than in developed economies.

The shortage of skilled and trustworthy administrators is generally recognized. Moreover, what even the best of civil

services can accomplish is circumscribed by the level of education, of morals, and of cooperativeness of its society. One
example of this constraint of a backward public on government administrators is tax collection. The difficulties of applying an income tax in backward countries (and even in some
not so backward countries) are great, and a number of other
types of tax are not much easier to administer.

If we concentrate on economic development as the over-
riding objective in underdeveloped economies, then one especially significant limitation on the effectiveness of government
in the economy must be made clear. Starting from a backward
state, development requires reconstructing society, overturning
customs, making traditional occupations and skills obsolete,
damaging some advantageous economic positions, relocating
economic activity, and causing other upheavals in the social
and economic structure. These changes involve costs, but in a
system of decentralized decision making, the costs are external
to the initiators (the beneficiaries) of change and are omitted
from the calculations. In a system of central calculation, these
external costs become internalized and enter into the calculations for economic policy.[15]

If central calculation internalizes both the gains and the
losses that are external to decentralized calculations, will the
net effect be stimulating or discouraging to development? The
answer obviously depends on the relative size of the external
economies and diseconomies. It is generally recognized that
cases of external economies in the strict sense are few and of
minor significance.[16] The external diseconomies of development, on the other hand, are extensive. The great changes in
the social and economic structure which development involves
will impose substantial costs on those whose social status,
occupation, or location is adversely affected. Thus the internalization of both external economies and diseconomies is highly
likely, on balance, to be discouraging to economic change.[17]

---

[15] See the discussion of internalization and its effects on growth in *ibid.*,
pp. 55–61.

[16] See Scitovsky, "Two Concepts of External Economies," *op. cit.*

[17] An amusing example of how internalization may backfire is provided
by S. K. Nath, *op. cit.*, p. 140. Nath, an advocate of central calculation

Is it not correct, despite the adverse effects on development, to take all gains and costs into account? It would be if (1) the gains and costs were correctly estimated and (2) finding an excess of gains over cost would lead to the adoption of the change. Unfortunately, in the case of economic development the calculation tends to fall down badly on both of these requirements. The fear of the unknown makes the losses appear greater and the gains smaller than they will prove to be. It is in this fact that the conservatism of the static society is rooted. Second, even where the net gain is recognized, the internalization of the calculation (that is, the concentration of decision and control in the government) empowers the losers to resist the change through the political process. Conceivably, the gainers could compensate the losers and buy their acquiescence. To some extent, such trading is a normal part of the operations of government. But in the case of the wholesale change of society involved in development, the high price demanded by those who fear change and the reluctance of the gainers (who are uncertain about the extent of their future gains) to offer compensation make bargaining extremely difficult. In consequence, internalization is likely to be highly discouraging to changes which will be of net social benefit.

Can the government centralize economic calculation and control and yet ignore the diseconomies of development? It can, in a political system in which the authorities can override the opponents of change. Hence the appeal of authoritarianism and the disenchantment with free institutions when the development decisions are concentrated in the hands of the government.

---

to stimulate development, quotes E. J. Mishan: "The divergence between private and social costs . . . provides a devastating criticism of the commercial criterion" for determining the allocation of resources. ("The Meaning of Efficiency in Economics," *The Bankers' Magazine,* June, 1960, p. 482.) However, Nath evidently did not note that Mishan is concerned with the external *dis*economies of economic development (destruction of the countryside, air pollution, congestion, etc.) and that, to Mishan, internalization is a means to slowing down development.

7 | planning for development: india

Among the underdeveloped countries, India offers one of the better opportunities to study a mixed-enterprise economy engaged in drawing up and attempting to implement comprehensive plans for economic development. In spite of some differences in economic conditions and institutions among these countries, the lessons of the Indian example are widely applicable.

WHAT KIND OF PLANNING?

In a country like India, where the word "planning" is invoked as a sort of blessing, the collection of all forms of economic regulation and activity by the government is often called "planning." Yet, although government controls and operations are indeed extensive and complex, only a part of the government program can be called "planning" in the more specific sense of a centrally calculated design for resource allocation. The formal planning process, as represented by the drawing up and implementing of the Five-Year Plans, makes a natural starting point for an examination of economic policy in India. However, the non-Plan economic policies also have major implications for the development of the economy and merit the same careful examination that is given to the Plans.

The Five-Year Plans are essentially outlines for the allocation of investment. Proposals are compiled for outlays on development programs by governments (center, states, and union territories) and for outlays on investment by the private sector. If the concept of "investment" is used in its broad sense to include, not only additions to physical capital, but also additions to intangible capital—knowledge, skills, information, and new social arrangements intended to increase economic productivity—the developmental outlays provided for in the Plan can all be considered investment.

The Plan outlays are given in broad sectoral groupings: agricultural programs, community development and cooperation, irrigation and power, industries and minerals, transport and communications, and social services. A further breakdown of outlays by a small number of subclassifications within each sector is provided. Finally the Plan discusses the proposed projects within each of the subclassifications and it lists specific projects, in so far as they are known.

The planned outlays and projects are arrived at by a process of consultation between the Planning Commission and representatives of the various ministries of the central government and state governments. The chief function of the Planning Commission is supposed to be to construct a pattern of investment which will be allocated in the light of the national objectives, which will in the aggregate fit within the limits set by the available resources, and which will be internally consistent in the sense that the investment in each industry will enable that industry to provide the additional inputs required by the other industries to fulfill their planned expansion.

The Plan also sets forth a list of production targets for specific goods and services. The targets may represent estimates of potential production arrived at *after* deciding on the allocation of investment (a procedure known as *planning forward*) or the targets may be calculated first and used as the basis for deciding on the allocation of investment (known as *planning backward*). In some cases, there may be no logical connection between targets and investment (planning sideways?). It is not clear what combination of these procedures the Indian planners have been using; it appears from the most recent effort, the Third Five-Year Plan, 1961–1965, that the movement is toward the planning-backward technique.

The implementation of the investment projects and the management of production are not the business of the Planning Commission but are left to the government agencies concerned with the public sector's part of the Plan and to the managers of the private sector. While the agencies and managers are subject to various pressures and controls through which the central government and the Planning Commission can seek to secure conformity to the broad outlines of the Plan, most economic management other than investment decisions is decentralized. The production targets, therefore, are not binding requirements imposed on producers. They are guidelines for the planners in allocating investment. The producers, whether public or private, exercise their discretion with regard to the quantity and composition of output and the techniques of production. This is not to say that producers have complete freedom of action, but only that, within the framework of the Plan and the extensive body of economic regulations, considerable scope for decentralized decision making is left.

The managers of the economy can be classified into the same three groups as in the United States or any other mixed-enterprise economy: the public non-enterprise sector—that part of the government concerned with producing services which cannot or should not be marketed (education, public health, national defense, etc.); the public-enterprise sector— publicly owned producers which sell their product; and the private-enterprise sector.

The public non-enterprise sector is operated on the same general principles as in other democratic countries. The Plan sets guidelines for five years, but it is the annual budgets which determine the amounts and types of projects which each agency will attempt to carry out during the year. Despite surface appearances, the budgeting processes in a country like India, having a formal apparatus of planning, and in a country without it, like the United States, are basically similar. In both countries the budget is the outcome of estimates of financial resources, forecasts of needs, weighing of alternatives, lobbying, pressures, and political considerations.

The public-enterprise sector, which includes railroads, communications, electric power, and a number of manufacturing enterprises, uses principally the public-corporation form of organization, though a few enterprises are organized as "departmental undertakings," under the direct control of the government ministries. The degree of autonomy that the managers of public enterprises should have is still undecided. The principles of independence from political interference and of operation in accordance with ordinary business calculations appear to be the starting point for formulating a policy with respect to the management of public enterprises,[1] but actual practice is extremely diverse. The setting of prices is generally in the hands of the supervising ministry or department, though in a number of enterprises the corporation management makes many of the pricing decisions. The ministries maintain control over capital expenditures. Decisions about inputs other than capital and about output are made by the corporation management with varying degrees of interference from above. The typical public enterprise, therefore, is a firm which, within the limits set by government pricing policy and control of the investment total, and subject to various regulations and *ad hoc* interventions, is expected to behave in a businesslike way, responding to market forces and maximizing profits or minimizing losses.

The private sector is hedged in by a greater variety of regulations and controls than is applied to private enterprises in the developed Western economies. Nevertheless, the basic characteristic of the private sector is that it is privately managed, relying in its calculations and decisions on the price signals of a market system.

The Indian economy is, therefore, planned with respect to investment. Other economic decisions are primarily in the hands of management, which follows the signals of the market though circumscribed by a variety of regulations and controls

---

[1] See Om Prakash, *The Theory and Working of State Corporations, with Special Reference to India* (London: George Allen & Unwin, Ltd., 1962); V. V. Ramanadham, *The Finances of Public Enterprises* (Bombay: Asia Publishing House, 1963).

and, in the case of public enterprises, by direct intervention from the controlling ministries or departments.

THE STRATEGY OF INDIAN PLANNING

Indian Plans are built upon a broad strategy. "Strategy" in this context means an investment program sketched in the most general terms and based on the identification of the main objectives and of certain crucial constraints.

the main objectives

The main officially stated objectives underlying the planning strategy are three.

Growth The Plan sets a target for the growth of national income. In the Third Plan, for example, the target for national income is a 30 percent increase over the five years, or just under 6 percent per year.

Reduction of unemployment A critically important characteristic of the Indian economy is its extensive chronic unemployment. The unemployment is in part visible and in part disguised or concealed (labor with no productivity, in the sense that it could be taken out of production without loss of output, given only some reorganization of the work).[2] Indian unemployment is predominantly structural, arising from an insufficiency of land, capital, knowledge, and skills to combine with the surplus labor, and is not due to inadequate demand for output.

---

[2] Doubts have been raised about the existence of any significant amount of concealed unemployment in agriculture, where most of it has been said to be. See Harry T. Oshima, "Underemployment in Backward Economies: An Empirical Comment," *Journal of Political Economy,* vol. 66, no. 3 (June, 1958), pp. 259–264; Theodore W. Schultz, *Transforming Traditional Agriculture* (New Haven, Conn.: Yale University Press, 1964). However, correctly or not, the Indian planners believe concealed unemployment to be extensive, and it is therefore a datum in designing the strategy for Indian planning.

In an economy operated by market criteria, the attack on unemployment would follow as a by-product of the program for accelerating growth. The increase in the rate of capital formation and the allocation of capital and labor to their most productive uses would, in the process of pursuing the growth objective, also draw some of the unemployed into production. By specifying the reduction of unemployment as an independent objective, the planners imply that policies may be pursued which will sacrifice some growth for a greater reduction of unemployment. The clash between the growth and employment objectives has, in fact, been evident in various employment-creating projects which reduce total output through a misallocation of resources.

One important example has occurred in the government regulation of the cotton-textile industry. Government policy has been to expand handspinning and handloom weaving, partly through direct encouragement and partly through restrictions on the mechanized textile mills. Encouragements to handwork have taken the form of credit, subsidies, and assistance in marketing and design. Restrictions on mills have included limitations on the expansion of spinning equipment, on the introduction of automatic looms, and on the output of certain types of cloth which are the main product of the handlooms.[3] It is generally agreed that the result of these efforts has been a misallocation of capital which has restricted the growth of cotton-textile production.[4]

The employment objective, in so far as it is independent of the growth objective, has only a redistributive purpose. It reduces total product for the sake of redistributing some of the product to those who would otherwise be unemployed.

A *"socialist pattern of society"* The third planning objective —a "socialist pattern of society"—is a highly pliable concept. It

[3] See Baditha Srinavasa Rao, *Surveys of Indian Industries* (London: Oxford University Press, 1958), vol. 2, pp. 22–30; George Rosen, *Industrial Change in India* (Glencoe, Ill.: The Free Press, 1958), pp. 162–174.

[4] See, for example, Amartya Kumar Sen, *Choice of Techniques* (Oxford: Basil Blackwell, 1962), appendix D, "The Ambar-Charkha as a Technique of Cotton-spinning," pp. 115–119.

includes equality of opportunity, social mobility, distributive justice, and diffusion of power; and it means whatever the user means by those terms. Since capitalist countries' lists of social objectives include the same terms, the label "socialist" may seem misleading; and to some extent it is. Presumably India will use a variety of means to achieve its "socialist pattern," and it is not necessarily committed to the means that socialism ordinarily implies, the public ownership of the means of production. Nevertheless, public ownership of productive enterprises is the core of the Indian program to establish the socialist pattern. In heavy industry and industries characterized by large-scale units, new development has been reserved solely for public enterprises. By assigning the major share of industrial expansion to the public sector, the Plan aims to reduce monopoly, the concentration of power, and inequality in the distribution of income. Public monopoly and public concentration of power are not considered to be problems.

Thus far, the authorities have considered the attainment of the socialist pattern to be consistent with the continuation of private enterprises in agriculture, trade, and light industry, and in firms established in industries which have subsequently been reserved for the public sector. It is quite possible that this formula for the coexistence of private and public enterprise will continue; the socialist objective is not a doctrinaire pursuit of public ownership, but a reflection of the Indian preoccupation with questions of distribution.

the constraints

The constraints which underlie planning strategy include such obvious items as the shortage of saving and the scarcity of arable land relative to the population. While manpower, in general, is not a constraint, administrative, technical, and decision-making skills are.

Two other constraints are perhaps even more critical, and they present more intractable problems. One is the shortage of foreign exchange. Economic expansion in India depends crucially on imports. A part of the capital goods and a part of the raw materials must come from abroad. In the short run, there is an irreducible import component of capital-formation and raw-material input. Thus, the amount of foreign exchange available for imports sets a limit on investment which cannot be overcome by merely increasing domestic saving. To permit an increase in productive capacity, an increase of saving must be accompanied by an increase of foreign exchange, except to the minor extent that capital can be created by crude techniques having no import component. The economic Plan, therefore, is limited in size by the foreign-exchange availability, and its shape is conditioned by the need either to increase exports or to provide domestic substitutes for imports.

Another critical constraint is the progress-stifling culture and organization of rural India. All efforts to bring "the agricultural revolution" to India quickly collide with this obstacle.

Indian farmers are, by culture, highly conservative about agricultural techniques, as well as most other matters. In part, this conservatism can be rationalized as a prudent avoidance of risk by people who have no reserves to fall back on should their venture with new methods fail. But the widespread reluctance to adopt innovations which have been well tested and demonstrated indicates that the resistance to change goes beyond mere prudence and that it has its basis in the conservative outlook typical of traditionalist societies.[5]

In addition to its attitude toward change, rural India suffers from a long list of deficiencies that impede agricultural progress. Illiteracy makes it difficult to communicate technical information to farmers. Local initiative in modern developmental projects is practically unknown. Suspicion of each other and of government authorities is deeply engrained in villagers' minds. The social structure of the villages is rigidly hierarchical. The power of the top level of the hierarchy has been con-

[5] India is a country of great diversity. Attitudes and customs vary regionally and among the many different castes and communities. Groups are found which are receptive to change, but the predominant characteristic of farmers is a conservative clinging to traditional ways. Examples of this attitude—refusal of farmers familiar with irrigation to take advantage of an increase in the availability of water, indifference to fertilization or new crops even after extended demonstrations of their advantages—have been gathered from many areas of India by Kusum Nair, *Blossoms in the Dust* (New York: Frederick A. Praeger, Inc., 1961).

sistently used in the past and continues to be used in the present to seize control of government programs for village development, to divert these programs to the ends of the few at the top, and to exclude the rest from benefit. This power structure has persistently frustrated efforts to inspire villagers to take the initiative in village improvement.[6] When credit facilities, which are thoroughly inadequate for Indian agriculture, are created in the villages, they are generally dominated by the upper stratum for its own benefit. If credit does seep down to lower levels, it is frequently misused for unproductive purposes, such as dowries and weddings.

Since the area under cultivation cannot be significantly increased, the growth of agricultural output depends upon increasing the yield of the land through improved techniques and multiple cropping during the year. The improvement of agricultural practices is seriously hampered by the culture and organization of the rural society. Consequently, agricultural progress depends upon a program for accelerating the renovation of rural society.

STRATEGY IN THEORY

It is highly probable that, if questions of political and administrative feasibility are set aside, economists putting together the objectives and constraints described above will not differ greatly about some principal elements in the best strategy for India's development. The chief elements in this probable consensus seem to me to be these:

1. Some increase is called for in total saving through government budget surpluses. The extent to which saving could usefully be increased is not great, since investment is limited less by lack of saving than by other shortages, such as those of foreign exchange and administrative and technical skills. Nevertheless, a case can be made for some net contribution by the government to total saving.

[6] See Walter C. Neale, "The Indian Peasant, the State, and Economic Development," *Land Economics,* vol. 38, no. 4 (November, 1962), pp. 281–291.

2. Capital formation can be increased, with no reduction in consumption, if the large supply of unemployed labor is put to work on capital projects that require relatively little capital. Roads and canals are examples of capital that can be constructed with labor and a small quantity of simple equipment. In order to convert unused labor into capital without straining the available resources, the employment of the unemployed must not be accompanied by an increase of total consumption. Taxation must be used to prevent those who were previously supporting the unemployed from increasing their consumption to the extent that they are relieved of that burden. Very roughly, the same consumer goods that sustained the unemployed will become their wages for creating capital. If total consumption rises somewhat, as seems inevitable, foreign aid may be obtained to provide the extra resources. If not, it may still be economically sound to divert resources from other investment to fill the consumption gap, provided that the investment sacrificed in that way is more than offset by the investment created through putting the unemployed to work on capital projects.[7]

3. The policies of increasing the rate of growth of output and reducing the rate of unemployment must be reconciled as much as possible. One approach is to encourage the use of the most labor-intensive techniques that can be employed without adversely affecting the growth rate. No general rules can be laid down concerning the proper degree of labor intensivity of the techniques of production or the commodities to be produced. Growth of output will ordinarily be maximized by choosing the techniques and the composition of output which, given the supply of the factors, the productivity of the factors, and the value of the products, will maximize the value of the current product. Provided that the prices of labor and capital reflect their costs in alternative uses and the prices of outputs reflect their relative values, ordinary profit-maximizing calculations by managers will lead to the choice of techniques and composition of output that will maximize current product. One

[7] See Ragnar Nurkse, *Problems of Capital Formation in Underdeveloped Countries* (Oxford: Basil Blackwell, 1953), chap. 2.

would expect that, in an economy with redundant labor, a relatively labor-intensive pattern would emerge.

Planning becomes involved in the factor-proportions question because the price of labor may not correctly reflect its alternative cost. Unemployed labor has a cost, in terms of alternative product, of zero, but the price of labor is necessarily above zero. In calculating costs, therefore, planners could use a *shadow price* for labor, measuring its social cost rather than its market price.[8] By the use of a shadow price which is lower than the market price of labor, a more labor-intensive set of production choices would be indicated.

Some increases in employment can be had, however, only at the cost of current output and growth of the economy. If structural unemployment persists when the economy is operating with the most efficient factor proportions, less efficient but more labor-intensive techniques can be introduced. Whether such a reduction of total income, in exchange for a more even spread of employment and income, results in a gain or a loss for society depends entirely on the society's values and preferences. Economists can only suggest that it should be possible to find a less costly redistributional device.

4. A prominent place in development strategy must be given to the foreign-exchange shortage. Where foreign exchange is in short supply and must be rationed, the true value of a unit of foreign exchange is greater than the value assigned to it by the official exchange rate. Because of the crucial role of imports in the investment program, the value of a unit of foreign exchange to the economy is likely to exceed its value at the official exchange rate by a very great deal. Planners, therefore, might base calculations involving foreign exchange on a shadow exchange rate which places a higher value on foreign exchange than the official rate does.[9]

[8] The price of capital may also fail to reflect its alternative cost, though there is no practical reason why interest rates in India should not correctly reflect alternatives. However, if they do not, planners could use shadow interest rates.

[9] This discussion presupposes that India will continue to find it inadvisable to reduce the price of the rupee enough to equate supply and demand in a free foreign-exchange market. It does not, however, rule out the possibility of some further adjustment of the exchange rate.

143

One effect of the shadow exchange rate will be to raise the value of a unit of product when it is exported compared to its value when purchased domestically. Consequently, these calculations should lead the planners to place increased emphasis on exports and on measures to stimulate exports.

A second effect of the shadow exchange rate will be to raise the cost of imports as calculated for planning purposes. The higher calculated cost of imports should lead to a planned shift of resources to the domestic production of substitutes for imports. In particular, the calculations based on the shadow exchange rate will indicate the economic desirability of expanding the production of capital goods to replace imported capital goods which constitute such a critical bottleneck in the investment program. The exact extent of the allocation of resources to the expansion of the capital-goods industries depends, of course, on several things: the extent of the foreign-exchange shortage, the possibility of easing it by increasing exports or by obtaining foreign aid, and the suitability of the economy's resources for the production of capital goods.

5. The keystone in the development strategy must be a program to modernize the culture and organization of the agricultural sector. The ultimate bottleneck in Indian growth is agricultural production. Efforts to increase the rate of investment quickly raise the demand for food; the great difficulty of restricting the rise in demand for food imposes a serious limitation on investment. Even the foreign-exchange constraint is subordinate to the agricultural problem, since the chief method of alleviating the foreign-exchange shortage—import substitution—requires heavy investment in the capital-goods industries, which is restricted by the food supply.

A further contribution of agricultural improvement to economic development will come through the expansion of markets for consumer-goods industries that will accompany a rise of farm income. Excess capacity already exists in a number of light manufacturing industries and further expansion in these lines would not be difficult. The limiting factor is consumer demand for manufactures, which cannot be increased much until agricultural production, the source of income of 70 percent of Indian families, is substantially increased.

Modernization of the agricultural sector cannot be accomplished only by investment in physical capital—irrigation, fertilizers, tools—or research in agricultural methods. These investments must be accompanied by a program to modernize the farmer. Not only are demonstration of and education in new agricultural methods required to enable farmers to adopt these methods, but a change in the traditional resistant attitude toward new methods must be induced in a preponderant proportion of the farm population. Certain other obstacles to the use of new methods—farmers' suspicion of the government; the fear of many farmers that they cannot depend on officials to supply water, fertilizer, and improved seed when these are needed; extortion of a fee by some petty officials for the use of the water—can be partially overcome by education which will enable farmers to defend themselves against official abuses, and by an overhaul of the rural power structure. When investment in agricultural facilities runs ahead of the preparation of farmers to use them, the result is the underuse of facilities that has been observed in many parts of India.

STRATEGY IN PRACTICE

Economic strategy as actually designed and implemented by the Indian government bears only a modest resemblance to the theoretical framework.

1. The net government contribution to saving is quite small. During the Second Plan (1956–1961), the excess of tax receipts over current expenditures plus the surplus of public enterprises amounted to 26 percent of the total public-sector Plan outlay, 18 percent of total investment, and 1.8 percent of national income. Government saving proposed in the Third Plan is 39 percent of the proposed public-sector Plan outlay, 30 percent of expected total investment, and 3.6 percent of expected national income. Nor do these figures represent a net contribution by government to total saving. The surplus of

government enterprises is only a substitute for, and is probably less than, the business saving that would have occurred if these enterprises had been private. The surplus on tax revenues is partly at the expense of private saving, especially in the case of taxes on personal and corporate incomes. Thus, even if the optimistic expectations of the Third Plan are fulfilled,[10] the government addition to total saving will be minor.

There are several good reasons why an increase of saving has been and should be a minor function of planning in India. The mechanical difficulties of increasing tax revenues are great. The administration of tax collection is understaffed.[11] Enforcement is inadequate.[12] Public resistance to taxation and ingenuity in evading taxes must be taken into account: Rough calculations using 1953–1954 data suggest that only about one-half of taxable nonsalary income is reported.[13] Further, the political hazards of a sizable increase in the tax program are serious. To go much beyond the present tax effort would require heavier taxation on the broad economic base—lower incomes and consumer staples—which would not only magnify the administrative problems but create political stresses that would threaten the democratic process.

An important aspect of the limited role of the government in saving is that an indiscriminate curtailment of consumption would be of dubious value for development. A cut in the consumption of most manufactured goods and services would merely leave capacity idle and release labor which, because of the extensive unemployment, is not needed for capital formation. The domestic resource which it is essential to mobilize for an expanded investment program is food. If food can be

[10] Estimates for the first three years of the Plan show government saving running far behind the Plan expectation. "Mid-term Appraisal of Third Plan," *Economic Weekly*, vol. 15, no. 50 (Dec. 14, 1963), p. 2046.

[11] Paul H. Appleby, "Meeting Future Personnel Needs," *Indian Journal of Public Administration*, vol. 2, no. 1 (January–March, 1956), p. 7.

[12] Paul H. Appleby, *Public Administration in India: Report of a Survey* (New Delhi: Government of India, Cabinet Secretariat, Organisation & Methods Division, 1953), p. 33.

[13] Nicholas Kaldor, *Indian Tax Reform: Report of a Survey* (New Delhi: Department of Economic Affairs, Ministry of Finance, 1956), pp. 103–105.

diverted to workers on capital projects, employment in capital formation can be increased. A tax program to accelerate investment must, therefore, be aimed at restricting food consumption to prevent excess demand for food when employment in capital formation is expanded. But a tax which would succeed in restricting food consumption is, from the viewpoint of both practical administration and politics, unthinkable in India today.

2. The strategy of converting the unutilized potential saving represented by the unemployed into realized capital formation has played little part in Indian planning. The ultimate impediment to such a program on a great scale is doubtless the lack of fiscal power for restraining the rise of demand for food that would accompany a major public works program. If consumer demand cannot be controlled, the public works program for the unemployed, like any other kind of investment project, is limited by the resources available for investment. However, the fact that there has not been full exploitation of wheat available from the United States as aid (except during famines) suggests that organization and administration, and possibly other inputs, are immediate limiting factors.

3. The strategic device of encouraging labor-intensive techniques by calculating with shadow wages that are lower than actual wages or by subsidizing wages is not used in Indian planning. In general, the presumption is that managers, public and private, will seek least-cost methods of production calculated on the basis of actual factor prices and factor productivities.

One explanation for this policy may be that the attempt to stimulate the use of more labor-intensive techniques is likely to affect the rate of growth adversely. A large component of total saving is the saving out of profits. The choice of factor proportions on the basis of shadow factor prices rather than actual prices will reduce profits. Unless the loss of saving resulting from the reduction of profits is replaced by increased tax revenues, total saving and total investment will be reduced. Because of the difficulty of increasing tax revenues in a country like India, the attempt to shift production techniques toward greater labor intensiveness by the use of shadow wages or wage subsidies would require a curtailment of the investment program.[14]

The planning effort to utilize the unemployed has been concentrated in the program for encouraging the village industries of spinning, weaving, handicrafts, and several other simple labor-intensive manufacturing activities. While some success has been achieved in increasing the employment and output of these industries, it is doubtful that this part of the Plan has contributed to the development of the economy. Village industries absorb unemployed labor, which is a net gain, but they also absorb capital and government administrative resources which could be used more productively elsewhere. In addition, village industries, in general, use more raw material relative to the value of output than factory production, because of wastage and the inferior quality of the output. To provide a market for village industries, restrictions have been placed on investment and on some types of output in textiles (as has been noted), in agricultural implements, and in several other industries which compete with village production,[15] so that the output of village industries is to some extent only a substitute for other output and not an addition. Finally, because of the limited taxing capacity of the government, the funds devoted to supporting the village industries represent a diversion of funds from other developmental outlays which, by all indications, would be more productive. The village-industry program probably contains portions which can be defended on efficiency criteria, but by and large it is a redistributive program which operates at some cost to economic develop-

[14] This argument against encouraging labor intensiveness at the expense of maximization of profits has been developed in W. Galenson and H. Leibenstein, "Investment Criteria, Productivity, and Economic Development," *Quarterly Journal of Economics,* vol. 69, no. 3 (August, 1955), pp. 343–370; M. Dobb, *An Essay on Economic Growth and Planning* (London: Routledge & Kegan Paul, Ltd., 1960). See also Gerald Sirkin, "Professor Dobb on Investment Criteria," *Kyklos,* vol. 17, fasc. 3 (1964), pp. 481–482.

[15] *Third Five Year Plan* (New Delhi: Government of India: Planning Commission, n.d.), p. 428.

ment. It is significant that the approach of the Third Plan is to reduce subsidies and discontinue sheltering of markets for village industries and, presumably, apart from such assistance in improving productivity as the government can give, to leave them to the test of the market.[16]

4. The foreign-exchange shortage has become a crucial element in the planning strategy. The planning method, however, has not been that of calculating costs and returns on the basis of a shadow exchange rate which reflects more correctly than the official rate the rupee value of foreign exchange. Instead, the approach has been the less precise one of proposing some stimulants for exports and giving preference in investment allocation to projects with low import content and industries producing import substitutes.

Until the Third Plan, little attention was paid to the need for export growth. From 1948 to the end of the First Plan in 1956, import demand increased only moderately, and the economy had substantial foreign-exchange reserves, so that no exchange pinch was felt. Far from encouraging exports, the government introduced export licensing and controls to limit exports of goods considered to be in short supply. During the Second Plan, the foreign-exchange shortage became acute. Reserves were exhausted, export earnings did not increase, and demand for imports of capital goods and raw materials soared. Nevertheless, no steps to stimulate exports were proposed at that time, and the tendency to restrict exports in favor of the home market continued.

In India the blame for the stagnation of exports was put almost entirely upon the stagnation of foreign demand for India's traditional products.[17] The prospects for any significant increase in exports were regarded as poor until such time as new export products in light manufacturing could be developed. It is doubtful, however, that demand alone is a sufficient explanation. Demand conditions for the types of products

[16] *Ibid.*, pp. 431–432.
[17] See Surendra J. Patel, "Export Prospects and Economic Growth: India," *Economic Journal,* vol. 69, no. 275 (September, 1959) pp. 490–506.

traditionally exported by India have been diverse. World demand for some of these products has been rising over the period covered by Indian planning, and, in those, India has generally failed to maintain her share of world trade.[18]

The lag in Indian exports must be laid in part to her noncompetitive prices in a number of products and the inadequate profit inducement to divert goods from the domestic to the export market.[19] This state of affairs appears to have been recognized in the Third Plan. Restrictions on exports to protect supplies for the home market have practically disappeared. The policy is turning toward measures to increase exportable surpluses and to subsidize exports through rebates on railroad freight rates and drawbacks on import duties paid on imports used in the production of exports.

The chief approach of the planners to the foreign-exchange constraint, aside from seeking foreign aid, has been to try to reduce import requirements through administrative controls. One of the guiding principles of investment allocation has been to favor industries with a low requirement for imported materials and industries which produce substitutes for imports. Much attention has been devoted to the development of heavy capital-goods production to reduce the dependence on imported equipment. The actual decision making has been impressionistic, a strong dose of import-saving bias mixed in with other investment criteria, rather than an attempt to optimize by exact calculation. Consequently, there has been considerable doubt that the investment choices have represented the best possible strategy. Will the capital stock be increased faster by expanding the capital-goods industries or by expanding the export industries in order to increase the capacity to import capital goods? Might not more foreign exchange be saved by importing capital goods to produce those import substitutes which can be quickly expanded than by investing in heavy

[18] See Benjamin Cohen, "A comment on S. J. Patel's Analysis of Indian Exports," *Indian Economic Journal,* vol. 11, no. 1 (July–September, 1963), pp. 37–46.

[19] Anne Krueger, "Export Prospects and Economic Growth: India: A Comment," *Economic Journal,* vol. 71, no. 282 (June, 1961), pp. 436–442.

capital-goods production which will yield results only after a long delay? [20]

In the absence of extensive calculations using prices that correctly value exports and imports, it is impossible to say how far the Indian Plan diverges from the optimum strategy in dealing with the foreign-exchange constraint. With respect to the much-debated question of investment in heavy industry, it seems probable—considering India's natural resources, its high demand for capital goods, and the prospective inadequacy of its export earnings even under the best export promotion program—that a fairly large investment in heavy industry is sound by ordinary productivity criteria. In other words, the planned investment in heavy industry more or less follows the pattern that would emerge from the profit calculation of a market system with tightly restricted imports.

5. Agricultural development is the *sine qua non* of economic growth and industrialization in India. Moreover, the government's role is more critical in agriculture than anywhere else in the economy: Outside the agricultural sector producers display the initiative to advance with little government assistance beyond the performance of the ordinary government functions required in any society, but Indian farmers will not progress without a great government effort to break the bonds of tradition and ignorance. Nevertheless, agriculture has not been given the central role in planning strategy that these facts warrant.

In the Third Plan, outlays for agricultural improvement are 16 percent of the total planned outlays.[21] While this is a step up from the 14.5 percent in the Second Plan, it is still a remarkably small proportion for the sector requiring the main government effort. Of this 16 percent, 7 percent is for major irrigation projects and 7 percent for seed and fertilizer research and distribution, minor irrigation, soil conservation and reclamation, plant protection, improved implements, and development of cooperatives. Not more than 2 percent is being

---

[20] See H. W. Arndt, "The Balance of Payments Argument for Priority to Heavy Industry," *Sankhyā, Indian Journal of Statistics,* ser. B, vol. 24, parts 3, 4 (February, 1962), pp. 265–276.

[21] *Third Five Year Plan,* table 3, p. 304.

devoted to the agricultural extension work, the demonstrations, and the education required to persuade and prepare farmers to use the new techniques and facilities that are being developed. The result has been that in the first ten years of planning, the yields per acre in India, which are among the lowest in the world, have risen very little. Most of the increased production has been obtained by increased acreage through irrigation, reclamation, and use of fallow land. The growth of agricultural production has barely kept ahead of the growth of population.

The 2 percent of the Plan devoted to agricultural extension and farmer training could be doubled with only minor trimming of expenditures on the major irrigation projects and industry. Since these additional outlays on agriculture would have virtually no import content, they would not compete for the most critically scarce input, foreign exchange. They would, however, compete for the attention of the government's scarce administrative and organizational capacity, and the expansion would require that the government divert some of its energy from tasks which can be handled by the private sector to tasks which only the government can perform.

The explanation for this relative neglect of agriculture can only be guessed at. Certainly it has not been for lack of awareness of the agricultural problem, which has been endlessly discussed. Part of the explanation must be the appeal and prestige of industrialization and large-scale projects compared to the unexciting work of nudging farmers. The unfamiliarity of intellectuals with rural society is a contributing factor. The poor visibility of the results of agricultural programs compared to the quick and showy results of industrialization is another. Perhaps the most important reason has been that, while the mechanics of building industry are well understood, no one knows much about how to modernize a traditional society. One can sympathize with an inclination to shy away from pouring large amounts of resources into the *terra incognita* of social change, yet it is precisely that kind of experimentation and risk taking which is supposed to be a major government function in economic development.

152

THE PLAN AND THE MARKET

This review of the strategy of Indian planning reveals that the Plans provide for little or no action on those policies by which theorists expect planning to improve upon the performance of the market. They do not provide for measures to secure a significant increase in total saving. They do not include a program for capital formation by use of the unemployed. They do not contain encouragements for labor-intensive techniques, except for programs to assist the village industries. (The latter, frequently wasting capital and administrative resources, and in the main supported by restrictions imposed on more efficient methods of production, are not quite what the theorists have in mind.) The Plans have fostered import substitution to meet the foreign-exchange shortage, but they have neglected the export side of the problem. Modernization of agriculture, which should be the core of the planning efforts, has been treated as an appendage.

The lack of resemblance between planning theory and practice appears not only in the broad strategy but also in the planning techniques. The calculations of external costs and returns, shadow prices, criteria for investment choice, models to ensure consistency between input supplies and output objectives, and other apparatus which bulk so large in planning theory play little or no part in Indian planning.[22] For all its planning terminology and trimmings, the Plan comes out

[22] Such attempts as have been made to use econometric techniques are exemplified by the very general pseudo-scientific model of P. C. Mahalanobis in "The Approach of Operational Research to Planning in India," *Sankhyā, Indian Journal of Statistics*, vol. 16, parts 1, 2 (December, 1955), pp. 3–62, which is supposed to have been influential in determining the strategy of the Second Plan. This model divides the economy into four producing sectors: investment-goods industries, factory-organized consumers' goods industries, household industries producing consumer goods, and service industries. Total investment is given. Capital and labor requirements per unit value of output in each sector are given. Two targets—an increase of employment of 11 million and an increase of national income of 5 percent per year—are set.

rather like the public capital budget of any non-planning private-enterprise economy, except that it is drawn up for five years instead of annually, and the public sector includes many enterprises which in other countries are left in private hands. Even the five-year period does not make the difference it might seem to, since the public outlays must, in the course of the Plan period, be revised in response to changing conditions.

There are excellent reasons why the Plans do not contain more planning. The government cannot mobilize the resources to do all the subsidizing that allocation by shadow prices would require. The data needed are not available. The country has a number of partially conflicting objectives, which include growth, employment, more equal distribution of income, more equal regional distribution of development, social welfare, security, and (I suspect) industrialization rather for the purpose of the national image than for purely economic considerations. These conflicts make it difficult to frame a coherent and consistent Plan which will also be generally acceptable. Political pressures must be taken into account, particularly with respect to the demands of the various regions for their share of new industries and public facilities.[23]

One-third of investment is arbitrarily assigned to the investment-goods industries on the basis of longer-run considerations. The problem is to allocate the remaining two-thirds of total investment among the other three sectors so as to achieve the targets.

The model does not consider whether the pattern of output conforms to the pattern of demand. It ignores foreign trade in its calculations. The setting of a growth target is an extremely dubious procedure. First, one may question whether the employment target should not be set aside to concentrate on raising the growth rate. More important, there is no reason why the problem as given should not be solved to *maximize* the growth rate rather than to aim at a particular rate. When the problem is solved in that way, it is found that the data permit a substantially higher growth rate with a quite different allocation of investment from the one proposed by Mahalanobis. See Ryutaro Komiya, "A Note on Professor Mahalanobis' Model of Indian Economic Planning," *Review of Economics and Statistics,* vol. 41, no. 1 (February, 1959), pp. 29–35.

[23] See Myron Weiner, *The Politics of Scarcity* (Chicago: The University of Chicago Press, 1962). Also, Wilfred Malenbaum, "Who does the

It is sometimes suggested that having most of the economy's production in the private sector has hampered the planning process. Evidence for this proposition, however, is lacking. In agriculture, it is true, there is little control over the investment or production decisions of the farmer; but the experience of countries with collective or state farms indicates that putting agriculture in the public sector is no aid to planning.

The private industrial sector, on the other hand, is subject to several direct controls which can be used to integrate it into the Plan in addition to the indirect controls over investment through monetary and credit policies. A license is required for any investment beyond a small minimum amount, whether for the establishment of a new enterprise or the expansion of an existing enterprise. Not a great deal is known about the functioning of the Licensing Committee, but it is supposed that its decisions are based on estimates of the need for additional capacity to meet Plan targets or other output objectives. The foreign-exchange requirements of an investment proposal, its location, the soundness of the venture, and the qualifications of the management are also taken into account. Inevitably, personal and political influences come to affect the decisions of the Licensing Committee.

Through licensing, the government has the power to make private industrial investment follow the rough guidelines of the Plan. Within the guidelines, the Licensing Committee must use its discretion. In practice, licensing responds (more or less) to supply and demand conditions, and its criteria resemble market criteria in many respects. Possibly licensing gives heavier weight to import saving than would entrepreneurs, because the

---

Planning?" in Richard L. Park and Irene Tinker (eds.), *Leadership and Political Institutions in India* (Princeton, N.J.: Princeton University Press, 1959), pp. 301–313. "Is this team—with people of such exemplary qualifications and under the leadership of the prime minister himself—apt to develop a plan in which the political requirements and objectives are realistically moderated by the technical and economic potentials? I think the answer is negative, and that is borne out by the experience of the last few years, the period of preparation of the second plan. Political and administrative considerations were dominant, economic realities notwithstanding [p. 310]."

prices of imports do not fully reflect their scarcity. Political pressures may on occasion run counter to economic considerations. But in the end the pattern of investment under licensing probably differs little, and not necessarily for the better, from the pattern that would emerge without licensing.

Licensing has greater significance in determining *who* will be permitted to invest than in determining *what* will be invested in. One argument frequently advanced for licensing is that it permits business opportunities to be reserved for the lower echelons of entrepreneurs, when otherwise investment would be dominated by a small group of industrial giants. On the other hand, it has been suggested that licensing has the contrary effect: The larger entrepreneurs have the resources to establish and maintain the "connections" to carry through the prolonged negotiations necessary to obtain licenses, while the lesser entrepreneurs cannot compete.

Against such minor accomplishments as licensing may have achieved must be set some serious drawbacks. The licensing procedure is used by entrenched members of an industry to lobby against the entry of new firms. Thus, it tends to have a restrictive and anti-competitive impact. Licensing favors the best-connected but not necessarily the best-qualified management. Indeed, a license frequently lies idle because the licensee is unable to promote the venture, while entrepreneurs who might be able to organize the enterprise successfully are thereby shut out.[24] Licensing imposes another costly lag on the decision-making process. Holders of licenses cannot, without permission, introduce new products not covered by the license. In general, licensing dampens entrepreneurial initiative, decreases competition, shelters less efficient entrepreneurs, and slows the responses of the economy, while apparently offering little by way of compensation.

The control over imports is the second major method by

[24] An instance of minor importance (except to the thirsty) of which I have been told is of a novice who obtained a highly prized license for a brewery. With the license as his only asset, he sought unsuccessfully, for several years, for a foreign collaborator who would put up all the capital for 49 percent of the stock.

which the government can direct private production. Almost all industries have import requirements (capital goods or materials) which are essential to their operation. Through its administration of import licenses, the government can regulate investment and production. Actually, this method of control is superfluous if licensing looks after the investment pattern and takes import requirements properly into account.[25] The chief function of import licenses is simply to ration foreign exchange. It has been convincingly argued that foreign exchange would be more correctly, quickly, and equitably rationed by allowing its price to clear the market.[26] This could be done by auction of the foreign exchange, by devaluation, or by higher import duties. Not only would rationing by price improve the allocation of foreign exchange, but it would improve economic calculations in general by valuing imports at prices more correctly reflecting their scarcity.[27]

Turning now from the design of the Plan to its implementation, we find a disparity between the planned and the actual achievements which has distressed many commentators. The growth, employment, and investment objectives have not been achieved. Output has fallen short of many production targets,

---

[25] A third control on private investment, the permit required to issue new securities, is superfluous. This capital-issue permit seems to follow automatically when the investment license and the import license have been granted.

[26] See J. Bhagwati, "Indian Balance of Payments Policy and Exchange Auctions," *Oxford Economic Papers*, new series, vol. 14, no. 1 (February, 1962), pp. 51–68; Bhagwati, "The Case for Devaluation," *Economic Weekly*, vol. 14, no. 31 (Aug. 4, 1962), pp. 1263–1266.

[27] The objection in India to this policy seems to be that it would raise prices. This would not be a substantial argument even if true. Actually, there is little truth in it. With the supply of an imported good fixed by import controls, the price of the good in India is determined by demand in the Indian market and not by the cost of the good to the importer.

After this was written, India devalued (by 36.5 percent on June 6, 1966). However, that adjustment was only enough to offset the recent rapid rise of prices (the wholesale price index rose 40 percent in the preceding four years) and still leaves the rupee substantially overvalued.

though some targets (nearly all in the private sector) have been exceeded. The phasing or timing of investment has come in for particular criticism.[28] If steel expansion had been begun during the First Plan, the steel bottleneck in the Second Plan would have been eased. A failure to provide for additional railroad cars led to a serious coal shortage in the steel mills at the beginning of the Third Plan. Expansion of the fertilizer industry was not begun early enough to provide for the Third Plan's increased emphasis on fertilizers. Electric power production has not always been in phase with industrial growth.

In part, the dissatisfaction with implementation results from a misunderstanding of the nature of the Plans. The specific aims of the Plans exceed what can be attained by the best management, given the available domestic saving, foreign exchange, skilled manpower, and administrative capacity. The Plans must be viewed as partially an expression of hopes and aspirations, rather than as wholly attainable goals. Moreover, the gift of prophecy which would permit accurate phasing without bottlenecks is not one of the resources accessible to planners. Planned and unplanned economies alike must meet uncertainty by being prepared to respond quickly and flexibly to signals of impending shortages or excesses.

Though it is unfair and misguided to demand full implementation of the Plans, the management of the Indian economy could nevertheless be considerably improved. One area for improvement is in flexibility of decision making and responsiveness to economic signals. The lag between management's perception of the need for an investment shift and the government's decision to make the shift, is generally excessive. The vicissitudes of the regulation of cement capacity will illustrate the point. In the mid-1950s the capacity of the cement industry was thought to have been somewhat overexpanded, and the government put a stop to further expansion. In a few years it became apparent to cement firms that the industry was heading for a shortage of capacity, but they could not get permission to expand. It was not until a severe shortage of cement

[28] See, for example, W. B. Reddaway, *The Development of the Indian Economy* (Homewood, Ill.: Richard D. Irwin, Inc., 1962).

had appeared that the government loosened the restrictions on expansion.[29]

A certain lack of responsiveness to economic developments is inherent in government operations. Not being entrepreneurs, government officials are unlikely to have the qualifications or the motivations to attune them to market forces. The centralization of decision making, the difficulty of delegating authority in government, and the unwillingness to accept responsibility delay action. Political haggling further slows down the process. Administrative practice may be better in some countries than others, but the relative slowness and inflexibility of government bureaus compared to autonomous enterprises (public or private) is a characteristic of all governments.[30] The obvious route to improvement is to shift economic decision making from political-bureaucratic control to enterprises guided and controlled by markets, unless there is a strong economic argument to the contrary.

Economic decisions can be improved not only in speed but also in rationality by a greater reliance on the price system. India since Independence has been passing through a phase of "controlitis," an outgrowth of misunderstanding of the working of the price system combined with undue faith in the wisdom and efficacy of government control.

Of the many unfortunate examples that can be cited, perhaps the most blatant is the food zones policy. In 1956 the government divided the country into zones and required permits for the movement of food grains across boundaries. The purpose was to prevent a zone whose demand for foodgrains exceeded its supply from "importing" grain from other zones and thus exerting upward pressure on prices there. The following year the Foodgrains Enquiry Committee enthusiastically recommended extending the policy to provide for cordons around the larger cities in the event of poor crops "to insulate the rest

---

[29] A similar cycle of overexpansion and overcontraction occurred in 1960–1963 in the control of sugar production. See "Sugar: Full Circle," *Economic Weekly*, vol. 15, no. 16 (Apr. 20, 1963), pp. 656–667.

[30] Witness the coin shortage in the United States in 1964 owing to the failure to expand the mint facilities, though the need was forecast in ample time.

of the economy from the pressure that these cities with high purchasing power might exert on the general supply." [31] The Committee further suggested that control of the railroads could be used for restricting long-distance movement of foodgrains. It reasoned that

> The experience of the last few years has shown that unfettered private trade tends to have highly undesirable effects in a situation like the one we are facing today. Foodgrains markets in India are essentially imperfect with the result that wide disparities in prices exist side by side. On the one hand, there are large metropolitan areas that often exert a considerable pull on markets in neighboring rural areas. On the other, there are pockets of scarcity acting as epicentres of price rise. Complete free trade in a basic essential like foodgrains under these circumstances tends to aggravate price fluctuations and to impede the course of planned development. [32]

The measures recommended have the effect of increasing the imperfections of the market and widening the disparities in prices. It is obvious that the restrictions on the movement of foodgrains, which can serve only to reduce aggregate welfare, are based on a misunderstanding of the most elemental economic principles. The restrictions, nevertheless, continue, [33] alleviated only by efforts of smugglers.

A variety of other interferences with the price system which reduce the efficiency of the economy can be pointed out. Controls over the price and use of basic commodities such as steel have no useful function. It has not been possible to control the price or allocation of steel, which is resold by those who buy it

[31] *Report of the Foodgrains Enquiry Committee* (New Delhi: Government of India, Ministry of Food and Agriculture, 1957), p. 98.

[32] *Ibid.*, p. 75.

[33] For example, groundnut oil prices at one point soared to a record high. "Near-famine conditions that these prices reflect are the result mainly of restrictions on the movement of groundnut and groundnut oil outside Gujerat and Uttar Pradesh." *Economic Weekly*, vol. 16, no. 38 (Sept. 19, 1964), p. 1540.

from the mills. The outcome has been the usual result of price control: uneconomic allocation of the product, encouragement of unnecessary middlemen, and diversion of profits from the producers (where it would serve as a stimulus to production) to the dealers (where it serves no purpose).

The distribution of fertilizers is another interesting case. It appears that "India's planners were faced by a pattern of chemical fertilizer consumption that had little relationship to socially-defined need. . . . Those who needed it most consumed it the least." [34] Fertilizer was presumably being bought by those who could make the most productive use of it. But "Against existing market patterns, the planners defined social need. For chemical fertilizers, these were derived from objective data on plant nutrient requirements." [35] Fertilizers were to be distributed without regard to productivity or farmers' demand. The objective of fertilizer distribution was evidently to be income equalization rather than income maximization. The result has obviously been an inefficient allocation of fertilizers. Indeed, the misallocation has been so acute that in some areas stocks of fertilizers are accumulating for lack of demand, while in other areas there is a shortage.[36]

PUBLIC VERSUS PRIVATE ENTERPRISE

In 1948 the Indian government adopted an Industrial Policy Resolution (revised in 1956) which established the rules with respect to public and private enterprise that have been in effect ever since. The Resolution lists a number of industries in which only the state may establish new enterprises (iron and steel, heavy plant and equipment, aircraft, shipbuilding). A second part lists industries which will be expanded mainly by the state but in which new private enterprises may also be

[34] J. Hart Walters, "Distributing Fertilizers by Administrative Order in India: An Example of Applied Economic Policy," *Indian Economic Journal,* vol. 6, no. 4 (April, 1959), pp. 443–444.

[35] *Ibid.,* p. 444.

[36] "Distribution of Fertilizers," *Economic Weekly,* vol. 15, no. 10 (Mar. 9, 1963), pp. 423–424.

established (aluminum, machine tools, basic chemicals, fertilizers, road and sea transport). Industries not listed are, in general, left to the private sector, though the state may start enterprises in this category if it chooses. Private industrial firms established before the Resolution have been allowed to continue.

Until recently the issue of public versus private has not been so lively as one might have expected. Peaceful coexistence prevails between public and private enterprise, and it is likely to remain peaceful as long as the relationship between them continues to be noncompetitive. The debate has become more active in recent years, not because of objections from the business community,[37] but because of a more widespread concern about the delays of the public sector in getting new enterprises under way.

Further, there is considerable concern in India about the efficiency of public enterprises. The issue of parliamentary and ministerial interference in the management of public enterprises is a dominant theme in discussions of Indian public administration. There is fairly general acceptance of the proposition that the efficient running of public enterprises requires an autonomous management operating on business principles, though there is no clear agreement on the precise boundaries of management's independence or on the extent to which management's calculations should be modified by broader social considerations. In practice, it has been extremely difficult to give autonomy to the management of public enterprises and to allow them to imitate private enterprises. The result has been that public managers are subject to the interference of government ministries, while long delays are introduced into the

---

[37] The faintness of the business community's criticisms of the government's restrictive policies toward business may seem surprising. In part it can be explained by the understandable caution of businessmen whose position in the society is precarious. More important is that the restrictive policies are not without some attractive compensation to established businesses. The licensing requirement for new firms, import licensing, and other regulations serve to limit the entry of competitors, thus providing the established firms with a more advantageous and secure position.

decision-making process, and the decisions are often based on dubious calculations.

These problems are illustrated by the experience of the Damodar Valley Corporation.[38] The DVC, a multipurpose river-valley authority, was established in 1948 by an act which "was to secure for it the fullest autonomy subject only to directions by the Central Government on matters of policy."[39] It quickly became clear that this autonomy would not, in fact, be respected, as the central government and the governments of the two states in which the valley is located immediately took a hand in the management. In 1953 the DVC recognized it would have to begin promptly to expand its electric-generating plant capacity to meet the rising demand for power. In April, 1953, the DVC requested the Ministry of Irrigation and Power to sanction the expansion. The request was not approved until February, 1957. During this long interval, the matter was batted about among the Ministry of Irrigation and Power, the Planning Commission, and the state governments of Bengal and Bihar. In the end it was approved substantially in the form in which the DVC originally proposed it.

Initially, the hesitation about permitting the expansion seems to have been based on a question about the priority which should be given to electricity. In a report in 1952, a Parliamentary Estimates Committee which assessed the DVC

> . . . felt that the D.V.C.'s work of flood control and irrigation had suffered on account of funds being diverted toward the establishment of the thermal station. The Committee noted with concern that a "secondary matter, namely, the erection of a thermal station", should have got priority over "the country's need in respect of food and agricultural produce."[40]

[38] This illustration has been reported in a detailed study: Parmanand Prasad, "The Expansion of the Bokaro Thermal Plant," in *Cases in Indian Administration* (New Delhi: Indian Institute of Public Administration, 1963), pp. 101–135.

[39] A. D. Gorwala, *Report on the Efficient Conduct of State Enterprises* (New Delhi: Government of India, Planning Commission, 1951), p. 32.

[40] Prasad, *op. cit.*, p. 109.

163

The Committee's views on priorities seem to have been influential when the question of expansion came up again in 1953.

Another difficulty was the relationship of the proposed expansion to the Plan. In July, 1954, a conference of the central government, Bengal, Bihar, and the DVC, was held.

> Although at this Conference of the Participating Governments the necessity for the expansion of power was admitted, in view of the First Five Year Plan coming to an end, it was decided that the matter should be deferred for inclusion in the Second Plan.[41]

The Second Plan was still two years away, but

> The Ministry of Irrigation and Power, perhaps, thought that as a project not included in the Plan has usually little chance of being approved by the Planning Commission, and as the First Plan was very near to its completion, it was no use pursuing the matter with the Commission.[42]

The end result of the long delay in approving the expansion was that the Calcutta area and the other areas supplied by the DVC suffered a severe shortage of electric power, which has restricted industrial production for years.

The DVC case illustrates a number of major obstacles to efficient management which are inherent in governmental control of enterprises. Most significant is the failure to use a sound method of calculating investment priorities. Whether or not capital should have been shifted from flood control and irrigation to power should have hinged on the relative productivity of capital in those uses; but the decision for a time was controlled by a parliamentary committee's view unsupported by proper analysis. Moreover, the decision should not have been restricted to a choice between flood control and irrigation, and

[41] *Ibid.*, p. 119.
[42] *Ibid.*

power. Investment in DVC power should have been competing for funds in the capital market with all other investment projects. Government control of investment by public enterprises has not provided a satisfactory substitute for the rate-of-profit calculation of autonomous enterprises.

A second generic problem of public enterprises illustrated by this case is the slow pace of decision making. Long after it was known that expansion of power was essential to prevent a critical situation in the industries serviced by the DVC, the decision was continually postponed. The division of the decision process into discrete five-year planning periods provides a special encouragement to postponement.

A variety of other difficulties is encountered in the public-enterprise sector. The rules of management are ambiguous. The enterprises are expected, in most cases, to make a profit, but not necessarily to maximize profits. The management may be expected to take into account various external costs and returns which will reduce profits, though at the same time the government's need for revenues creates pressure to increase the earnings of public enterprises. In this state of affairs, profits are an inadequate test of the efficiency of the enterprises, but no other test is available.

The insistence on public development of certain industries frequently retards their growth. This effect is particularly noticeable in those cases where foreign capital and technical assistance can be readily obtained by private firms but not by the government.[43] Another type of delay occurs when a new industry which is not covered by the Industrial Resolution, such as petrochemicals,[44] arrives on the scene, and its development must be held up while its allocation between the public and private sectors is debated.

The establishment and supervision of industry absorb a large portion of the organizational and administrative capability of the government. This unnecessary load on public admin-

---

[43] The development of the fertilizer industry is an example. See "Fertilizer Programme Flops," *Economic Weekly,* vol. 15, no. 19 (May 11, 1963).

[44] "Petro-chemicals: Public versus Private Sector," *Economic Weekly,* vol. 13, no. 50 (Dec. 16, 1961), pp. 1851–1852.

istration detracts from the government's performance of its essential functions.

The restraint of the private sector in favor of public enterprise imposes economic costs which cannot be taken lightly. The purpose of restraining the private sector—said to be to promote the "socialist pattern of society"—is obscure. How the diffusion of power will be achieved by concentrating industry in government hands, and how equality of opportunity or social mobility will be improved by enlarging the public sector, is not obvious. And the effect on the distribution of income will be trivial.

Quite possibly, continued experience with the costs and gains will lead to eventual rethinking of the present policy.

LESSONS OF THE INDIAN EXPERIENCE

India provides one of the better-documented examples of a proposition which holds for all economies that have attempted centralized planning: The formal models derived from theory have little relation to what governments want, or are able, to do. The experience of countries like India teaches that their economic management does not need and cannot benefit from comprehensive centralized calculation and control. On the contrary, what is needed is a clearer and narrower definition of the government's economic role which will permit the government to concentrate on its essential functions and free it from duties which it performs less well than the market.

As things now stand, India is merely repeating the history of its economic development as it was before the introduction of planning. From the late nineteenth century to Independence, industrial production grew at a respectable and fairly steady rate.[45] The key factor in stimulating industrial growth seems

[45] See D. B. Meek, "Some Measures of Economic Activity in India," *Journal of the Royal Statistical Society,* vol. C, part 3 (1937), pp. 363–388, which presents an index of industrial production (cotton textiles, jute, woolens, paper, breweries, iron and steel) that grew at about 3.4 percent per year from 1896/1897 to 1932/1933. Also D. R. Gadgil, *The Industrial Evolution of India in Recent Times* (London: Oxford University Press, 1944); Mahinder D. Chaudhry, "National Income

to have been protection of the domestic market. Even during the 1930s, Indian manufacturing output continued to increase as protection was extended. The great economic lag was in agriculture, which was virtually stagnant during the period, and which, because of its preponderance in total output, accounts for the appearance of overall economic stagnation. The rapid response of manufacturing to increased demand when protection was applied suggests that, had agricultural incomes risen, the resulting increase of demand would have generated an even faster rate of industrial growth. Hence, the backwardness of the agricultural sector accounts both directly and indirectly for the poor record of economic growth before Independence.

This preplanning pattern is continuing under the current Plans. Industrial production has been rising strongly (at about 7 percent per year), while agricultural production has barely been keeping up with population growth. There has been no lack of entrepreneurial talent or willingness to expand industrial capacity; rather, the government has been actively engaged in restraining private entrepreneurship. The main impediments to a faster rate of industrial growth have been foreign exchange, the backwardness of agriculture, and the misallocation and delays arising from the many government interferences with the market system.

Small signs are appearing that, in the light of her experience, India will modify her policies. To accelerate the development of industries like aluminum and fertilizers, which were previously reserved for the public sector, private development has been permitted. In 1964, controls on the price and allocation of steel were partially removed after an inquiry into the inefficiency of the system of controls. A continuation in the direction of leaving to private initiative the tasks which private initiative can perform and concentrating the government's limited resources and administrative capacity on the tasks which only the government can perform—especially the modernization of agriculture—will speed India's development.

---

8 | guidelines for the visible hand *

In the decade following World War II, the long swing of economic analysis toward an idealized view of the state's role in the economy reached a peak. The experience with and intensive study of the market economy had produced an understanding of its realities which was not matched by an equally widespread understanding of the realities of the state's economic performance.

Exaggerated ideas of the omniscience of the government could always be found among theoretical economists.[1] But in the 1930s and 1940s, the abstract models based on the government as a perfect economic calculator became ever more widely accepted as a description of potential reality. Unchecked by confrontation with experience, the literature on planning flourished.[2] In general this literature was character-

---

* This chapter was published in *The Philippine Economic Journal,* vol. 5, no. 1 (1966).

[1] See, for example, the notion that the government can foresee the obsolescence of equipment better than private entrepreneurs and consequently can reduce the rate of obsolescence through planning, in Maurice Dobb, "Economic Theory and the Problem of a Socialist Economy," *Economic Journal,* December, 1933.

[2] "The literature on planning has the great advantage of moving in a fairy world. Capitalist economy is something real. . . . In the fairy world all is perfect and faultless." Gustav Stolper, *This Age of Fable* (New York: Reynal & Hitchcock, Inc., 1942), p. 64.

ized by the implicit assumptions that the objectives of the society were agreed upon; that the central collection and processing of economic information involved no major difficulties; that the government possessed unusual powers to foresee the future; that government personnel were disinterested automatons, more "rational" in their decision making than private individuals, and seeking only to maximize the social welfare; that economic calculation and "politics" could be kept in separate compartments.[3]

Among experienced economists in the established centers of economic study, this dream-world view of the state-guided economy was generally recognized for what it is: a product of naïveté or doctrinaire ideology or abstract model building for analytical purposes. But among intellectuals untrained in economics and among the young economists of the newly developing areas, there was a marked propensity to accept the planning literature as the basis for practical policy.

The past twenty years have seen a large number of countries

[3] For a representative example of this genre, see Carl Landauer, *Theory of National Economic Planning*, 2d ed. (Berkeley, Calif.: University of California Press, 1947). His concept of planning is comprehensive: "Planning can be defined as guidance of economic activities by a communal organ through a scheme which describes, in quantitative as well as qualitative terms, the productive processes that ought to be undertaken during a designated future period [p. 13]."

Landauer's planning begins with an inventory of inputs. "We must know how much arable land, how much pasture, how much workable mineral deposits of every kind, how much equipment of every description, and how much labor of every skill we have at our disposal before we can choose what we want to produce [p. 36]." Consumers' preferences are to be respected; therefore ". . . we must find out their preferences [p. 37]." "From its engineering advisers the planning board can obtain all the information it needs about the technical procedures in producing goods for the satisfaction of the consumers. It will also be advised about the required amounts of material, equipment, and labor [p. 37]." With this data in hand, the planning board solves all the equations for an optimum allocation of resources. Problems of conflicting interests and the impact of the political process on the state's economic decisions are easily handled: ". . . [a] clear dividing line must be drawn between technical questions of planning, which should be decided by independent nonpolitical experts, and all political decisions, which must be made by elected representatives [p. 249]."

embark on programs of planning. In this comparatively brief time, enough experience has been gained to dispel many of the optimistic illusions. Far from promising optimum solutions, today's practical planner is happy if the outcome is passable by even rough standards. Thus:

> If . . . [instead of formal mathematical models] one is trying to study an actual economy, paucity of data and lack of time combine to force one to make many assumptions intuitively or arbitrarily, and also to make "reasoned guesses" of things which ought logically to be calculated much more elaborately: whole ranges of theoretical possibilities are likely to be unexamined, and one cannot hope to say with conviction that a proposed Plan is definitely "the best"—it is hard enough to be confident that it is consistent and broadly on good lines. One hopes that one can distinguish the important issues, and concentrate on careful consideration of them; and—perhaps most important of all—one does not attempt to fix immutably (or even to specify) every detail for every year, but rather tries to orient the analysis so as to get guidance on action which must be taken now or in the near future.[4]

However, despite the extensive recent experience and its contribution toward greater realism, the discussion of the government's role in the economy remains remarkably disorderly. With neither the enthusiasts nor the skeptics about government able to describe with any precision what they advocate, charges of "laissez fairist" and "collectivist" are exchanged, and the differences between them are made to appear greater than they really are.

The purpose of this book has been to seek a set of proposi-

---

[4] W. B. Reddaway, *The Development of the Indian Economy* (Homewood, Ill.: Richard D. Irwin, Inc., 1962), p. 63. See also Oskar Lange, "The Role of Planning in Socialist Economy," *Indian Economic Review*, vol. 4, no. 2 (August, 1958), pp. 1–15, for an experienced planner's views of the limits of centralized decision making.

tions about the organization of economic decision making which will clarify the discussion of the agenda of government. I suggest that the following propositions, on which reasonable men should be able to agree, will serve that purpose.

1. The market and the state are both imperfect decision makers. Some of these imperfections are correctable or partially correctable, but both market and state have defects which are inherent and which cannot be corrected. There is as little to be gained from contrasting the real market with a model of a perfect government decision-making machine as there is from contrasting the real behavior of government with a perfect market mechanism.

2. In all situations where economic welfare does not offer a clear basis for choice between the market and the government, those who value individual freedom should prefer the market on the ground that it offers a wider dispersion of power. Those with a distaste for individual freedom should hold the opposite preference.

3. In any system which uses markets, there should be no objection in principle, from any party, to government programs aimed at improving the functioning of the markets. There may be controversy over how a program should be carried out or whether it is justified by its results, but the principle of including market improvement in the agenda of government should not be an issue.

Thus, the propriety of government policies to improve information, to increase competition, and to reduce impediments to the mobility of inputs and outputs should not be a subject of ideological debate. Most important, the question of stabilization policy should be eliminated from the debate.

Stabilization policy provides a most striking example of misunderstanding about the role of government in the economy. It has been hailed by some and attacked by others as an example of the replacement of the market system by government control. Yet the principal instruments of stabilization policy (fiscal and monetary adjustments) need not involve any direct interference in markets. These instruments are methods of improving the conditions within which markets operate. There may be questions about the mechanics of implementing stabilization policies, but about the consistency of these policies with a market system there need be no dispute.

4. The government must be responsible for the production of those services which are, by nature, non-marketable.

5. A pragmatic approach is needed in deciding on specific cases where the government may replace the market because of market defects. In these cases, it must be kept in mind that government decision making has its own inherent defects. The choice between two defective methods is not one which can be made on principle, but only by an evaluation of their relative defectiveness in each particular case.

It would be ideal to be able to quantify the net gains or losses of each government intervention as compared to the performance of the market. It seems improbable, however, that much precision in this type of measurement can be achieved. But it is possible that rough guidelines can be developed. Where the gains of a program are clear, where there is broad agreement on objectives, where administration requires the enforcement of a small number of general (non-arbitrary) rules, where frequent adjustments of the rules are not required, and where valuable attributes of the market such as competition are not adversely affected, the program is likely to make a positive contribution. (The control of water pollution might be an example.) Where the gains are problematical, where the objectives are ambiguous, where administration requires many specific or arbitrary decisions, and where competition or the motivation for efficiency is impaired, the value of the program will be dubious. In all cases the government's administrative capability must be taken into account. A type of intervention which yields net benefits in a society having competent administration may yield net losses in a society having serious administrative deficiencies.

6. If the term "planning" is used to refer to the three government activities listed above—improving the operation of markets, producing non-marketable services, and intervening in specific cases of market defects—there should be no controversy over the acceptability of and need for planning in any market economy. When, however, "planning" is used in its stricter sense to mean centralized decision making by the gov-

ernment in replacement to any extent of the market mechanism, there is a basis for controversy.

If we can agree to agree on these six propositions, the issues about planning that remain to be discussed can be reduced and sharpened.

The first of these is the question of planning in its strict sense: centralized calculation and direction of the economy. The preceding chapters have presented the theoretical arguments for the proposition that centralized government decision making cannot be optimal, and the reasons why in practice centralized calculation and administration are a less efficient method of managing an economy than a decentralized market system. While some may still want to dispute the case, the many recent defections of centrally planned economies of Central and Eastern Europe to the market system—the Soviet Union is only the latest example [5]—have undermined their argument.

If "planning" does not refer to the design of a comprehensive program for government direction of the economy—if, in other words, decentralized decision makers in a market system are to make the bulk of the economic decisions—then it must refer to the design of a program for the basic government functions. These basic functions, as noted above in this chapter, are: (1) to produce services which cannot be produced by the market mechanism; (2) to correct specific market defects by taxation, subsidy, regulation, or similar market interventions; (3) to improve the working of the market by such measures as increasing the mobility of resources or improving the information available to decision makers.

The substantive issue that remains is not so much one of defining the government's functions as of choosing the best method for performing those functions. Drawing up a five-year plan of public receipts and expenditures, aimed at growth tar-

---

[5] On September 29, 1965, the Central Committee of the Communist Party adopted a resolution approving measures for improving the management of industry. These measures include greater independence for the managers of enterprises and the use of profits as a guide to enterprises. *The Current Digest of the Soviet Press,* vol. 17, no. 38 (Oct. 13, 1965), pp. 16–17.

gets and other social objectives and based on forecasts of available inputs, technology, and performance of the private sector, is only one approach to the formulation of a program for the government's functions. Countries that do not draw up formal multiyear plan documents, and countries that draw them up but do not use them, have their own ways of formulating their public programs. Ordinarily these methods are based on annual budgets modified in the course of the year as events unfold.

The difference between these two methods should not be exaggerated. A five-year plan cannot be rigorously adhered to; it must be subject to revision, either periodically or as circumstances demand. On the other hand, the annual budget and the programs and projects of the various government agencies, in countries that do not put together long-term plan documents, are necessarily based on estimates for a longer period than the year ahead, whenever investments or programs with long preparation times are involved. Nevertheless, there are important differences. The formal multiyear plan, if it has any operational significance, is resistant to frequent review and modification. Frequent revision is taken as a sign of the defectiveness of the plan and the incompetence of the planners. Consequently the multiyear plan, unless it is a purely intellectual exercise without operational significance, exercises a constraint over policy during its life. By comparison, the annual budget, by limiting to one year the government's commitment to specific future actions, and by limiting its reliance on forecasting, leaves decision making substantially more adjustable.

What are the advantages of drawing up a comprehensive plan? One advantage is supposed to be that it ensures that the objectives, the assumptions, and the forecasts on which government economic policy is based will be well thought out and will be made explicit.[6] There is no reason, of course, why these things cannot be done in any system of government policy

---

[6] See, for example, Jan Tinbergen, *Central Planning* (New Haven, Conn.: Yale University Press, 1964), pp. 42–43, where the characteristic features of a planned policy are listed as: the use of forecasts, the explicit formulation of general aims, and coordinated action instead of random action by government agencies.

making, and there is no insurance that they will be done in any system of government policy making. The same difficulties afflict all systems: The objectives are numerous and frequently in conflict, the assumptions are tenuous, the forecasts are shaky. The plan must be compatible with, or at least must not exclude too emphatically, the diverse objectives, assumptions, and forecasts of the government decision makers and administrators, if the planners hope to influence policy. Consequently, it is doubtful that, in practice, the objectives, assumptions, and forecasts are made significantly more explicit or coherent in a formal plan than they are in a system of government decision making without a plan document.

The second advantage expected from the formal planning procedure is the coordination of the various branches and agencies of the government. Under conditions of highly reliable forecasting or near certainty about the future, coordination can be improved by drawing up a plan. But under conditions of uncertainty and unreliable forecasting (which is the predominant state in economic affairs), precisely the reverse proposition holds: Plans are prone to hamper coordination. When developments are difficult to predict, coordination depends upon fast reactions and readjustments. To the extent that the long-term plan commits decision makers to a given set of policies, it reduces their freedom to adjust.

Even if planning can make a contribution to coordination, it is doubtful that that accomplishment is all to the good. Perfect coordination may look neat and be aesthetically satisfying and yet be a slower way of making economic progress than less orderly methods. A high degree of coordination frequently requires restraining the more dynamic elements of the economy, which, if allowed to unbalance the allocation of resources temporarily, will pull the laggards forward.[7] Moreover, the pursuit

[7] This point is the central argument of Albert O. Hirschman, *The Strategy of Economic Development* (New Haven, Conn.: Yale University Press, 1958). See also Charles E. Lindblom, "Tinbergen on Policymaking," *Journal of Political Economy*, vol. 66, no. 6 (December, 1958), pp. 531–538, which emphasizes the conflicts of values in a society and the need for groups to explore their own values, and the effects of alternative policies on those values, in the process of policy making. "Conflicts cannot always be bargained out in advance of the

of perfect coordination by a central authority stifles the competitive spirit among government agencies, with the consequent loss of some of the drive for better performance that would result from the efforts of each agency to expand its own program more rapidly than the others. Finally, the cost of coordination, in the form of a more unwieldy and cumbersome administrative process, rises with the pursuit of more perfect coordination. The gains sought from coordination will at some point be outweighed by the resulting loss of efficiency.

A third achievement claimed for planning is that it increases the information available to decision makers in a decentralized system. Purely "indicative" planning, for example, consists solely of a set of forecasts of production and government policies intended to enable entrepreneurs to improve their decisions. No one will dispute the virtues of better information for decision makers, but one may seriously question whether the long-term plan documents add to the supply of useful information. There can be no assurance that a plan, even if ostensibly kept unchanged, will actually be fulfilled. Moreover, a plan must always be viewed as subject to revision. Conceivably, the announcement of a plan promising some particular rate of long-term growth might instill a "growth" mentality in otherwise static-minded entrepreneurs. But it seems doubtful that the mere announcement of a plan is likely to change entrepreneurial thinking in the absence of experience and facts sufficient in themselves to have already convinced entrepreneurs of the probability of long-term growth. Whether or not indicative plans are drawn up, the decision maker must pro-

---

policy decision, and bargaining sometimes waits until unpredictable conflicts of policy become apparent. Under these circumstances, to ask that policies be consistent is to stultify policy-making. Where different agencies of government counter one another with opposing policies without bargaining, an agency's formulation of a policy inconsistent with some other agency's policy may be the only possible mechanism of adjustment among interests defending various values. It can be conceded that inconsistency is a cost; but it is a cost well worth incurring where, for problems too complex for central comprehension, there is no better way to represent all important values than by putting some autonomous power or authority into the hands of each of a large number of agencies [p. 538]."

177

ceed in much the same way: On the basis of the same sort of general information as is available to planners, plus his specialized knowledge of his own activity, each decision maker must make his own judgment of the most probable outcome and be prepared to revise his judgments and decisions as economic requirements evolve.

In opposition to the positive contributions claimed for the formal plan document stand some observable negative results that I have cited in the preceding chapter. The most costly of the adverse effects of the formal plan document is the inflexibility which it introduces into public decision making. Once decisions for a five-year period have been published, the inclination is strong to postpone reexamination or revision until the next plan, except under the pressure of a crisis. The competence and even the purpose of the planning commission may be called into question if the plan is frequently revised. Also, the plan provides a convenient excuse for postponing the reopening of controversial matters. Finally, it is frequently argued that the usefulness of the plan as a basis for informed forecasts will be damaged (as it unquestionably will be) if it is subject to revision. Where such considerations are prevalent in government thinking, the tendency will be to twist economic decisions to match the forecasts rather than to meet the fundamental criteria of economic policy.

A second unfortunate consequence of the formal plan document is that it leads the government to assume the central direction of functions which are better left to the market. By creating the illusion of a capacity to eliminate uncertainty and a capacity to calculate and implement a grand optimal "solution" for the allocation of resources, planning frequently inspires governments to undertake programs which they would have left to decentralized decision making had they more realistically appraised the problems of uncertainty and the difficulties of central calculation and administration.

The issue of the method of formulating public policy comes down to a choice of orientation toward one of two techniques. One is the technique, just discussed, which seeks to make maximum use of centralized calculation, coordination by centralized direction, and forecasting. The alternative technique uses decentralized decision makers, whose actions are coordinated by their mutual adjustments, intercommunications, and bargaining ("horse-trading") with each other. The results of these interactions may be compiled in a budget, with conflicts temporarily resolved by executive or legislative actions (which themselves reflect mutual adjustment and horse-trading among various interests). But the decisions are not final in the sense that they fix a pattern of government policies and allocations for a specific period; they are subject to continuous reexamination and adjustment in the light of subsequent experience. Because this method emphasizes adjustability, it does not place heavy reliance on forecasting.

In defining these two techniques, I do not mean to imply that governments employ either type in a pure or extreme form. Five-year plans are not the product solely of a group of detached optimum-calculating experts; the pressures of diverse and conflicting interests inevitably have some effect in shaping the plan. Nor can the plan be rigidly followed; compromises and revisions must be made, however belatedly. (Unfulfilled plans are a type of revision.) On the other hand, governments that do not employ the planning apparatus do apply some degree of central supervision and coordination and base their decisions on forecasts, depending on the nature of the decisions and the confidence felt in the forecasts. Nevertheless there is an unmistakable distinction between a system which aims at the maximization of centralization and reliance on forecasts, and a system which recognizes the virtues of decentralization and seeks to minimize the reliance on forecasts.

Before the two methods can be properly compared, it is necessary to recognize that the "non-planning" method is actually a systematic analytical procedure for determining public policy. This method, which has been named *incrementalism*,[8] proceeds by a series of steps or adjustments chosen by the comparison of a limited number of alternatives, and in the same process explores the values of the members of the society and revises the ends of policy in the light of what is learned about those values. Accepting the facts of inadequate data, un-

[8] Charles E. Lindblom, "Policy Analysis," *American Economic Review*, vol. 48, no. 3 (June, 1958), pp. 289–312.

certainty, conflicting values, and ignorance about values, the incrementalist rejects the planner's vision of a blueprint of optimum means to reach predetermined ends; he prefers, instead, a system which feels its way toward an improved position by successive adjustments.

Whether the planned or the incremental approach provides better public policy is a matter for empirical investigation. The award cannot be summarily given to planning simply because it appears to be more orderly or more "scientific." The key question is: Which method is more effective? In a world of imperfect knowledge and imperfect men, the apparently more disorderly method is frequently the more effective one.[9]

The experience of nations shows an inverse relationship between the compilation of a formal plan document and the quality of the country's economic performance. For example, a survey of nine case studies [10] finds the weakest results among the most serious formal planners (Burma, Pakistan, India) and among those which would like to be serious formal planners (Iran, Nigeria), and the most successful results among those countries which make only perfunctory gestures at planning (Japan, Mexico), or have shifted substantially from a centrally planned toward a market-type economy (Yugoslavia). The ninth country (England) has made a relatively poor showing in economic growth both before and since its recently adopted exercise in drawing up plans.

Such evidence does not constitute a scientific test, but it is suggestive. It suggests that economic performance has little or nothing to do with the kinds of long-term plans that governments prepare. The evidence of these and of other country studies points to the proposition that the rate of economic progress is positively related, not to the extent of centralized calculation, but to the enterprising character, the determina-

---

[9] For some interesting illustrations of this principle, see Albert O. Hirschman and Charles E. Lindblom, "Economic Development, Research and Development, Policy-making," *Behavioral Science*, vol. 7, no. 2 (April, 1962), pp. 211–222.

[10] Everett E. Hagen (ed.), *Planning Economic Development* (Homewood, Ill.: Richard D. Irwin, Inc., 1963).

tion, and the ability of great numbers of decision makers and managers in both the private and public sectors who must implement as well as make decisions.

The difficulty of seeing that incremental policy making is an orderly and coherent procedure, and that comprehensive long-term plans, when not empty exercises, are impediments to efficient economic management, may explain the curious proclivity of the United States government to urge planning upon other countries. During the West German reconstruction period in the early 1950s, American officials argued for more investment planning,[11] fortunately without much success. Underdeveloped countries in particular are pressed by the United States government to draw up plans. Thus a congressional committee states:

> In the presentation of the administration's new AID program special emphasis was given to the need for development planning as against the financing of isolated projects which are not formulated with the framework of a broad economic program, and with only sporadic or discontinuous relationships between the various external economic assistance agencies and the individual developing countries.[12]

[11] "Particularly the ECA representatives, concerned with the most effective use of American aid, laid stress on the need for investment planning." Henry C. Wallich, *Mainsprings of the German Revival* (New Haven, Conn.: Yale University Press, 1955), pp. 157–158.

[12] U.S. Congress, Joint Economic Committee, *Economic Policies Toward Less Developed Countries*, 1961, p. 31. The quoted statement is qualified in the following two sentences: "It must be recognized, however, that a development plan, no matter how well conceived, does not constitute a magic key or formula to successful growth. Most developing countries of the world have something which they call a development plan, but in most cases they are not based on an adequate survey of resources, on longrun projections of demand for commodities and services, on a properly balanced and consistent set of output and investment requirements, and on a realistic appraisal of the requirements for increased exports and how to achieve them [pp. 31–32]." However, this qualification concerns, not the use of planning procedure, but only the technical qualities of the plan.

181

This congressional policy statement does recognize, however, that in some types of economies comprehensive plans have little to contribute and may even be harmful:

> At the other end of the spectrum there are a few developing countries such as Mexico, where development is progressing satisfactorily and where formal 3- or 5-year overall plans which employ elaborate statistical techniques may not be appropriate. This does not mean that planning for certain sectors of the economy is not necessary in all countries, even in the United States, but there are countries where government and private firms and financing agencies have achieved a relatively high degree of sophistication in determining investment priorities on the basis of the operation of the price system and free market forces. For such countries formal overall planning of the type represented by the Indian 5-year plans are not only unnecessary for successful growth, but might introduce elements of inflexibility into the system which would actually inhibit growth.[13]

That is to say, in countries where public officials and private entrepreneurs have the initiative and ability to make and carry out rational economic decisions, the formal plan document is not needed.

There remains only to add that in countries without such public officials and private entrepreneurs the formal plan document does not work.

[13] *Ibid.*, p. 32.

index

Adams, Walter, 64n.
Administrators, shortage of, 130–131
Advertising, outdoor, 16
Aesthetic values, preservation of, 80, 84–85
Agenda of government, 7–8
  six propositions for, 173–174
  (See also Government economic policy)
Agricultural price support, 66
Agriculture, backwardness of, 167
  Indian, 140–141, 151–152
  modernization of, 144–145
    plans to modernize, 153
    task of Government in, 167
    stagnant since nineteenth century, 167
AID and plan documents, 181
Allocation of resources, 45, 46
Anti-competitive effect of licensing in India, 156
Appleby, Paul H., 146n.
Arndt, H. W., 151n.
Automobile, 85–87
Autonomy in public enterprises, 136–137

Backwardness, attack on, 117–122
  through land reform, 122
  through population control, 122

Backwardness, attack on, through public entrepreneurship, 120–121
  defined, 115
Bain, Joe S., 11–12n.
Banfield, Edward C., 118n.
Bargaining, 59
Bauchet, Pierre, 91n.
Bauer, Catherine, 87n.
Bauer, P. T., 24n.
Baum, Warren C., 90n.
Baumol, William J., 22–23n.
Beckman, Rune, 95n.
Belgium, 94
Benefits, social, 45–46
Bengal, 164
Bentham, Jeremy, 7
Bergson, Abram, 102–103n.
Berliner, Joseph S., 98n.
Bettelheim, Charles, 75n.
Bhagwati, J., 157n.
Bihar, 164
Bjerve, Petter Jacob, 95n.
Blight, urban, 80–81
Bokaro Thermal Plant (see Damodar Valley Corporation)
Brasilia, 90n.
Britain, 94, 180
Budget, performance, 61n.
Budgets, annual, in India and America, 135
Bureaucracy, 62, 129

183

Burke, Edmund, 7
Burma, 180

Calculation, divergence between private and social, 16
Calcutta area (*see* Damodar Valley Corporation)
Canaday, John, 90*n*.
Capital formation, 123
Capital formation in India, 142, 153
Capital formation in Indian planning, 147
Capital-funds market, 25
Capital stock, 37, 40
Cement industry in India, 158–159
Central authority, 3–4
Centralization (*see* Decentralization and growth)
Centralized planning, 68–73
  lessons about, from Indian experience, 166–167
Chaudhry, Mahinder D., 166–167*n*.
Cities, planned, Brasilia, 90*n*.
  unplanned, 89–90
City, characteristics of, 88
  crime in, 88
  function of, 87
City planning, failures of, 88–89
Cohen, Benjamin, 150*n*.
Cohn, Stanley H., 111*n*., 113*n*.
Cole, Margaret I., 7
Collective use, 9
Collectives, 66
Collectivism, 4
Collectivist, 171
Competition, 9–14, 57, 172
  government attitude toward, 62–64
    Interstate Commerce Commission, 64
  government restriction of, 63–64, 66
  imperfect, 11, 14, 47, 67
  innovational, 14
  inter-industry, 12

Competition, international, 12
  inter-product, 11
  intra-industry, 12
  oligopolistic, 14
  potential, 12, 13
  price, 14
  pure, 13, 14
Competition among buyers, 23
Competition in India, 162*n*.
Competition and the political process, 63
Concentration, of economic power, 5
  of production, 11–12
Conflicts of objectives, 119, 154
Conservation, of open space, 87
  of resources, 17*n*.
Consumer sovereignty, 19
Consumers' surplus, 28–29
Consumption, 19–20, 34–35, 39, 41
  lifetime, 31, 33–34
Controls, Indian, on private sector, 153–157
Cooperatives, 66
Corruption, public, 66–67
Costs, decreasing, 27–29, 47, 52
  external, 19
  non-market, 16–17
  social, 45–46
Cottage industry, 66
Cotton-textile industry, Indian, 138
Czechoslovakia, 71

Dahl, Robert A., 43, 45
Damodar Valley Corporation, 163–165
Data, Indian, 154
Decentralization and growth, 127
Decreasing-cost industries, 27–29, 47, 52
Defense, national, 9
Demand, excess, 48
  inelasticity of, 20
  for investment, 103
Democracy, 5, 59–60
Destabilizing speculation, 22
Devaluation in India, 143*n*., 157

Development, strategy for India, 141–152
Dictatorship, 59–60
Diminishing returns to research, 104
Distribution of income (*see* Income distribution)
Dobb, Maurice, 50–52*n.*, 100*n.*, 101*n.*, 148*n.*, 169*n.*
Durbin, E. F. M., 3*n.*, 45*n.*

Economic development, equalizing effect of, 27
Economic growth in Soviet Union, 102–113
Economic policy (*see* Government economic policy)
Economic power, dispersion of, 6–7
Economic welfare, 172
Economies of scale, 11, 20
Eddington, A. S., 67*n.*
Einhorn, Henry A., 12*n.*
Elasticity of demand, 13
Electric power production and Indian planning, 158
  (*See also* Damodar Valley Corporation)
Elliott, John E., 44*n.*
England, 94, 180
Entrepreneur, private, 21, 25, 156
  public, 20, 25
  (*See also* Entrepreneurship)
Entrepreneurial buoyancy, 105
Entrepreneurship, 20
  administrative skills of, 120
  improvement through land reform, 122
  personality traits required, 119–120
  public, 20, 25, 120–121
  shortage of, 120–121, 128
  willingness to take risk, 25
  (*See also* Entrepreneur)
Estate motive, 37
  private, 38
  social, 38

Excess demand, 48
Exchange rates, flexible, 23
  (*See also* Shadow exchange rate)
Exports, Indian, 151, 153
  controls on, 149, 150
  stagnation of, 149–150
External benefits, 38, 104
  and costs and centralized planning, 74
External costs, 19, 83
  or benefits in land-use planning, 79–81
External diseconomies, 17, 52
External economies, 17, 18, 50, 101, 127
  and diseconomies, internalization of, 131–132
  of saving, 37
Externalities, 16, 47

Fainsod, Merle, 60*n.*, 109*n.*
Farrell, M. J., 23*n.*
Feiss, Carl, 80*n.*
Fertilizer distribution in India, 161
Fertilizer industry in India, 165*n.*, 167
Fiscal policy, 15, 48, 172
Fisher, G. H., 76*n.*
Fleming, J. Marcus, 95*n.*
Flexible exchange rates, 23
Flood control, 9
Food zones policy in India, 159–160
Foodgrains Enquiry Committee, 159–160
Forecasting, 3, 4, 10, 49, 176, 179
  and central planning, 75–76
  government, 49
  by speculators, 22
Foreign capital, 124
Foreign exchange, 124
  in India, 139–140, 143, 149–151
Foreign grants and loans, 123

Foresight, 19
France, planning in, 90–93
Franks, Sir Oliver, 43n.
Freedom, individual, 172
    personal, 5
Friedman, Milton, 22n., 33n., 63n.

Gadgil, D. R., 166n.
Galenson, W., 148n.
Gan, Herbert J., 81n.
Garden cities, 81–82
Gellhorn, Walter, 63n.
Gerschenkron, Alexander, 106n.
Golden age, 42
Goldsmith, Raymond W., 106n.
Gorwala, A. D., 163n.
Government economic policy, 5–9,
        55–77
    criteria for, 61
    objectives of, 58–60
    role of the state, 7–8, 169–182
Government enterprise, effect of, on
        industrial growth, 165
    obstacles inherent in manage-
        ment of, 164–165
Government-directed economy, 64
Granick, David, 98–99n.
Grossman, Gregory, 103n.
Growth,
    as objective of Indian planning,
        137
    balanced, 125–130
        (See also unbalanced, below)
    in Sovet Union, 102–113
    unbalanced, 128–130
Growth rate, natural, 41

Hagen, Everett E., 118n., 180n.
Hamberg, D., 14n.
Harbeson, Robert W., 28n.
Harr, Charles M., 85n.
Harrod, R. F., 36
Hirschman, Albert O., 129n., 176n.,
        180n.
Historical values, preservation of,
        80, 84–85

Hoffman, Stanley, 92n.
Hungary, 71

Ignorance, consumer, 19
Import substitutes, Indian policy
        favoring, 150, 153
Imports, in India, 151
    control of, 156–157
    prices of, 156
    restriction of, 30
Income, 26–27, 138–139
Income differences, equalizing
        functions of, 26–27
Income distribution, 26, 138–139
Income redistribution, 26–27
Incrementalism, 179–181
Independence, economic, 5
India, 133–167, 180
    Five-Year Plans, 133, 134
        to allocate investment by in-
            dustry, 134
        description of, 134
        implementation of, 157–158
        as production targets, 134
        reasons for limitations of, 154
        Third Five-Year Plan, 135
Indicative planning, 91–93, 105,
        177
    descriptive of, 91–92
    functions of, 91–92
Industrial Policy Resolution, India,
        161–162
    effect of, on growth, 165
Industrial production in India,
        growth of, 166–167
Infant-industry argument, 30
Information, 9–10, 19–20, 47–49,
        67–68, 101, 127, 172
    in centrally planned economies,
        72
    of consumers, 19
    and multiyear plans, 176
Interdependence, 16–18
    among consumers, 16
    between consumers and produc-
        tion, 16

Interdependence, market, 18
  non-market, 16, 18, 47
  among producers, 17–18
Interest, 34
International trade, 74–75
International transactions, 29
Interstate Commerce Commission, 64
Inventions, 14n.
Inventories, 65
Investment, demand for, 103
  pattern of, under licensing in India, 156
  timing of, under Indian planning, 158
Investment decisions, 18
Iran, 180
Irrationality, consumer, 19
  public and private, 65–66
Israel, 116
Italy, 94n.

Jacobs, Jane, 81, 87n.
Japan, 112–113, 116, 180

Kaldor, Nicholas, 105, 146n.
Keyes, Lucille Sheppard, 64n.
Keynes, J. M., 7–8
Khrushchev, N., 65n.
Kindleberger, Charles P., 92n., 93n.
Komiya, Ryutaro, 154n.
Koopmans, Tjalling C., 51n.
Krueger, Anne, 150n.

Labor-intensive techniques, 142, 147
  Indian, 153
Labor markets, 10
Lafayette Square, Washington, D. C., 85
Laissez faire, 4, 171
Land reform, 27
  as way of improving entrepreneurship, 122

Land-use planning and the automobile, 89
Landauer, Carl, 170n.
Lange, Oskar, 69n., 171n.
Lauterbach, Albert, 43n.
Lee, James E., 84n.
Leibenstein, H., 148n.
Less developed economies, speculation in, 22
  (See also Backwardness; Underdevelopment)
Lewis, W. Arthur, 118n.
Licenses for imports in India, 157
Licensing, 63
  in India, 155–157, 162n.
  drawbacks of, 156
Licensing Committee in India, 155
Lindblom, C. E., 43, 45, 176–177n., 179n., 180n.
Lockwood, William W., 113n.
Lundberg, Erik, 95n.
Lyashchenko, Peter I., 106n.

McCarthyist period, 6
Mahalanobis, P. C., 153–154n.
Malenbaum, Wilfred, 154n.
Mangahas, Mahar, 24n.
Marginal-cost pricing, 28
Marginal utility, 33–34
  diminishing, 33n.
  increasing, 33n.
Marginal-utility function, 34–35
Marglin, Stephen A., 38, 40
Market, 16, 172
  attempts of government to improve, 15
  for capital funds, 25
  and food supply in India, 159–160
  inherent defects in, 16
  simulated, 69–70, 75n.
  (See also under Non-market)
Market defects, and government policy in India, 173
  and planning, 47

Market interdependence, 18
Market mechanism, 46
Market system, 27, 173
  (*See also* Price system)
Markets, 8
  government programs to improve
    functioning of, 9, 172
  labor, 10
  security, 10
  (*See also* Market; Non-market)
Meade, James E., 17n., 21n.
Meek, D. B., 166n.
Mehta, G. L., 5n.
Mexico, 116, 180, 182
Misallocation of fertilizers in India,
  161
Mishan, E. J., 132n.
Mixed-enterprise economy, 133
Monetary policy, 15, 48, 172
Monopoly, 11, 13, 63
  in India, 139
  natural, 11
  public, 14
  regulation of, 20
Monopoly policy, anti-, 12
Monopoly power, 12–13, 48
Monopsony in agriculture, 24
Moore, Barrington, Jr., 60n.
Moorsteen, Richard, 107n.
Motive, estate, 37
Mumford, Lewis, 87n.
Myint, H., 106n., 115n.

Nair, Kusum, 140n.
Nath, S. K., 128n., 131–132n.
Navigation, aids to, 9
Neale, Walter C., 141n.
Nehru, Jawaharlal, 2
NEP, 71
Netherlands, The, planning in, 90,
  94
Neuberger, Egon, 95n.
Nigeria, 180
Non-Agenda of government,
  7–8

Non-market interdependence, 18
Non-market products, 8–9, 173
Non-market valuations, 74
Non-planning (*see* Incrementalism)
Norway, planning in, 90, 94–95
Nove, Alec, 99n., 109–110
Nurkse, Ragnar, 126n., 142n.
Nutter, G. Warren, 12n.

Objectives, conflict of, 119
  in government economic policy,
    58–60, 83
Oligopolist, 13–14
Optimizing, 3
Oshima, Harry T., 137n.
Ownership, private, 53
  public, 53
Oxnam, Bishop Bromley, 43n.

Pakistan, 180
Park, Richard L., 155n.
Parks, 9
Patel, Surendra J., 149n.
Performance budget, 61n.
Petrochemicals in India, 165
Phelps, Edmund, 41n.
Pigou, A. C., 36
Pittsburgh, redevelopment of, 43,
  44
Planning, 43
  centralized, 101
    information for, 68, 72–74
    lessons of Indian experience
      with, 166–167
    versus decentralized, 53
  definitions, 44–45
  and forecasting, 3–4
  Indian, 133–167
    for agricultural development,
      152
    Planning Commission, func-
      tion of, 134, 135
    strategy of, 137, 153
      objectives of, 137

Planning, indicative, 91–93, 105, 177
  land-use, 79–90
  and the automobile, 85–87
  misunderstanding about, 2–4, 6
  non-price system of, 52
  and the price mechanism, 52
  Soviet, 97–102
  total versus partial, 53
  urban, 80–81
  (*See also* France; Incrementalism; Netherlands; Norway; Plans; Sweden; Yugoslavia)
Planning backward, 134, 135
Planning forward, 134
Planning program of basic government functions, 174
Plans, advantages of, 175–176
  contrasted with annual budgets, 175
  disadvantages of, 175–176
  and economic performance, 180, 182
  experience of countries with, 175
  multiyear, 133
  (*See also* Planning, centralized)
Poland, 71
Polanyi, Michael, 69, 71*n.*, 111
Police protection, 9
Pollution, 16, 173
Popper, Karl R., 67*n.*
Poverty, 27
Powell, Raymond P., 107*n.*
Prakash, Om, 136*n.*
Prasad, Parmanand, 163*n.*
Prebisch, Raúl, 4*n.*
Price control of steel in India, 160–161
Price discrimination, 29
Price mechanism, 51
Price system, 21, 51–53
  in France, failure of, 93
  in India,
Price system, in India,
  and foodgrains, 160
  government interferences with, 160
  misunderstanding of, 159
  (*See also* Cement industry in India; Electric power production and Indian planning; Food zones policy in India)
  (*See also* Market; Markets; Prices)
Prices, 16, 18, 46
Primary uncertainty, 51, 76, 101
Private economy, defects in, 67–78
  objectives of, 56
Private enterprise, 55
Private entrepreneurs, 21, 25
  and government in India, 162
Private sector in India, 135–136
  restraint of, 166
Production, conspicuous, 111
Profit calculation in centralized planning, 72
Profit criterion, 56, 61–63
  in Soviet Union, 98–99
Profits in government enterprises in India, 165
Prohibition, 19
Public administration, 173
  in India, 165–166
Public enterprise, 25, 57–58
  in India, 135–136, 161–166
    autonomy to managers of, 136–137
    Damodar Valley Corporation case, 163–165
    efficiency of, 162
    government interference with, 162
    setting of prices by, 136
Public entrepreneurs, 20, 25, 120–121
Public non-enterprise sector in India, 135

Public ownership, 14, 139
 (*See also* Public enterprise; Public entrepreneurs)
Public policy (*see* Government economic policy)
Pye, Lucian W., 70n.

Quality of products, 10, 99

Railroad regulation, 64
Ramanadham, V. V., 136n.
Rao, Baditha Srinavasa, 138n.
Raup, Philip M., 122n.
Recto, Aida E., 24n.
Reddaway, W. B., 158n., 171n.
Rehn, Gösta, 95n.
Reichenbach, Hans, 76n.
Research, basic, 17
 and external benefits, 104–105
Resource, free, 17
 shared, 14n.
Resource allocation, 45–46
Resource mobility, 9, 15
Resources, 17n.
 emergency reallocation of, 21
 misallocation of, 13
Risk, 21, 24–25, 47, 65
 cost of, 25
 reduction of, 20
Risk as argument for public entrepreneurship, 121
Roads, 9
Robbins, Lionel, 21n., 70–71n.
Robinson, Joan, 41n.
Rosen, George, 138n.
Rosenstein-Rodan, P. N., 125–126n., 127
Ruggles, Nancy D., 28n.
Russia, 116
 (*See also* Soviet Union)
Ruttan, V. W., 24n.

Sanitation, 9
Savage, L. J., 33n.

Saving, 19–20, 25n., 31–42, 47, 103, 124–125
 compulsory, 31, 37
 contribution by Indian Government, 145
 external economies of, 31, 37
 government intervention in, 35
 joint, 41
 optimum, 31
  (*See also* Saving plan, optimum-, 33–37)
 private rate of return on, 35
 social rate of return on, 31, 36
Saving in India, 139, 141, 153, 155
Saving plan, optimum-, 33–37
 (*See also* Saving, optimum)
Schultz, Theodore W., 137n.
Scitovsky, Tibor, 17n., 18, 19n., 50, 126n., 131n.
Secondary risk, reduction of, by government, 127
Secondary uncertainty, 51–52, 64, 76, 101
 in a government-directed economy, 64
Security markets, 10
Selling costs, 14n.
Sen, Amartya Kumar, 38n., 138n.
Sertic, Victor R., 95n.
Shadow exchange rate, 143, 144, 149
Shadow factor prices, 147
Shadow price for labor, 143
Sheahan, John, 91n., 93n., 126n.
Shils, Edward, 72n.
Simulated market system, 69–70, 75n.
Sirkin, Gerald, 104n., 148n.
Slums, 81
 unslumming of, 81n.
Social security programs, 37
Social estate motive, 38
"Socialist pattern of society," 138–139, 166
Solow, Robert M., 41n.
Soviet Union, 4, 65, 71, 116

Soviet Union, growth of capital stock of, 107–108
  growth rate compared to Japan's, 112–113
  NEP, 71
  planning in, 97–102
  Reforms of 1861, 106
  shortage system, 108
  surplus labor, 107
  technological lag, 107
  totalitarian control, 108–111
Soviet Union and market system, 174
Speculation, 24
  destabilizing, 22–23
  stabilizing, 22–23
Speculators, forecasts by, 22
Srinivasa Rao, Baditha, 138n.
Stabilization, 9, 15, 48, 172–173
Stabilizing speculation, 22–23
Steel in India, expansion, 158
  price and allocation controls, 167
  prices, 160
Stigler, George J., 67n.
Stockfisch, J. A., 19n., 76n.
Stolper, Gustav, 169n.
Stolper, Wolfgang F., 75n.
Streeten, Paul, 126n.
Subsidies, 51–52
Subsistence wage, 30
Suburbs, 85–86
Svennilson, Ingvar, 95n.
Swan, T. W., 41n.
Sweden, planning in, 90, 94–95

Tax collecting, 131
Taxation, in India, 142, 146–147
  progressive, 26–27
Taxes, 51–52
Technological knowledge, foreign, 125
Technological progress, 14n.
Telser, Lester G., 22n.
Time preference, 34, 36–37
Tinbergen, Jan, 175n., 176n.
Tinker, Irene, 155n.

Town and Country Planning Act of 1947, 85
Trade restrictions, 75
Trottenberg, Arthur D., 1n.
Tullock, Gordon, 40n.

Uncertainty, 20–21, 36, 65, 76–77
  and forecasting, 76
  primary, 51, 76, 101
  reduction of, 20–21
  secondary, 51–52, 64, 76, 101
    in a government-directed economy, 64
  in Soviet Union, 99
Underdeveloped, defined, 116
Underdeveloped countries, 30, 133
  (See also Backwardness)
Underdevelopment, attack on, through accelerating capital formation, 123
  by domestic saving, 124–125
  by foreign grants and loans, 123
  by private foreign capital, 124
  increased foreign exchange, 124
  technological knowledge, 125
  limitations of government in overcoming, 130–132
Underemployment, 30, 47
Unemployed labor in India, 142, 147–148
Unemployment, 48
  in India, concealed, 137n.
  reduction of, as planning objective, 137–138
Urban blight, 80–81
Urban planning, 80–91
Urban renewal programs, 87
Utility function, 34–35

Village industries in India, 148
Viner, Jacob, 23n.
Virgin lands scheme, 65

Wallich, Henry C., 181n.
Walters, J. Hart, 161n.
Webb, Beatrice, 7–8
Weiner, Myron, 154n.
Welfare economics, 26, 28
Wellisz, Stanislaw, 90–91n., 93n., 94n.
West Germany, 94, 181
Weststrate, C., 94n.
White, Leonard D., 23n.

White, Morton and Lucia, 82n.
Wiles, P. J. D., 72, 103n.
Wright, Frank Lloyd, 43

Yamey, B. S., 24
Yugoslavia, 70–71, 95–97, 180

Zoning, 52, 80, 83–84